Margaret Powell

Albert,
MY CONSORT

London
MICHAEL JOSEPH

First published in Great Britain by Michael Joseph Ltd
52 Bedford Square, London, W.C.1
1975

© 1975 by Margaret Powell

ISBN 0 7181 1402 7

Set and printed in Great Britain by
Northumberland Press Ltd, Gateshead
in Granjon type, eleven on thirteen point,
and bound by James Burn at Esher, Surrey

I gratefully acknowledge the permission of Mrs George Bambridge and Eyre Methuen Ltd. to quote an extract from 'Tommy' from *Barrack Room Ballads* by Rudyard Kipling.

To dear Albert, the one and only who could have put up with me; for all his love, and for always being there.

Chapter 1

The sterling qualities of Queen Victoria's Albert, the Prince Consort, were not recognised, or appreciated, by the majority of the British people. They had a deep distrust of all Germans, not without cause as eventually it turned out. But to my Albert's grandfather, Queen Victoria was the personification of everything a queen ought to be; and her husband, Albert the Good, a great man. He held these sentiments all his life. So much so, that although Queen Victoria and her Albert were no longer alive when my Albert was born, his grandfather persuaded his daughter to call this son, Albert; and one of Albert's brothers, Redvers—after Sir Redvers Buller of 'Ladysmith' fame. But then, Albert's grandfather, who had been a soldier in the Regular Army, was an ardent patriot. He believed in his Queen and Country. He considered that to be born an Englishman was the greatest blessing that life could bestow.

The hardships suffered by a regular soldier of those days, revolting food and living conditions, degrading punishments, all for a shilling a day, he had accepted as part of a soldier's lot, of serving one's country. The contrast between the ordinary rankers and the élite class of officers seemed nothing to him. It just had to be.

Albert's parents left their home town in Smallheath, Birmingham, when Albert was four years old. But Albert often went back to stay with his grandparents.

'Why only you? Why not one of your two brothers or five sisters?'

But Albert doesn't know why. Perhaps the others had no wish to stay with grandparents. Or maybe they wanted only Albert as he was a quiet boy and a good listener. He still is. Has to be, with me for a wife. In any case, he deliberates so long over a reply that by the time he thinks of an answer I have started on another subject. That's why his answers often seem so irrelevant to the questions. I remember on one occasion I bought some potatoes and complained to Albert that they were bad scrapers. Half-an-hour later, as we were eating them, he suddenly remarked, 'It's because they're not English.'

What can you do with a man like that?

'My grandfather,' said Albert, 'in fine weather used to sit on the wall at the end of the alley where he lived. This place was known as "Pops", because of a little general shop where the kids would gather to buy bottles of pop on a Sunday morning. Grandfather, with his other old cronies, all smoking foul-smelling clay pipes, would sometimes sit for hours, never saying a word. But occasionally, and I always tried to listen, they would talk of events of long ago as though it was only yesterday; of the Crimea, and South Africa.'

What Albert wanted to hear was tales of heroic deeds, blood and thunder, battles won and battles lost: all the excitement of chasing the enemy. But the old men never talked of such things; perhaps they had forgotten the dangers. When they spoke of the Crimea, it was about the bloody climate, the stinking hot summer, and the icy winds, snow and hurricanes of the winter; of sleeping on the bare ground without covers; or, when they had tents, fighting off the biggest rats in the world, and the fleas, millions of them; of how they had to march on a diet of salt pork and dry biscuit, dying of thirst; of the day they marched, when, what with all the men that collapsed on the way, and all those who threw away their equipment because they were too weak to carry it, the fields looked as though a battle had been fought. And they remembered Joe, or Bill, who had an arm or leg amputated where they lay, because there was no room in the hospital.

'Above all,' said Albert, 'they talked of their mates who had died, not of wounds, but of cholera and dysentery and the bloody diarrhoea; nowhere to go, no decencies, nothing but heat, cold, vermin and muck.' But the old men weren't blaming anybody for their hardships. They were an inevitable part of a soldier's life.

When Albert somewhat timidly spoke of the mistakes of the

Crimea, his grandfather just smiled. 'It couldn't be helped, son. Everyone was mad. Us infantry with thirst and fever. Our generals with power.' He either didn't know, or didn't care, about the incompetence of Lord Raglan and the enmity of the two principal officers. They were the bloody cavalry—nothing to do with the foot-sloggers.

And at the end of a soldier's life, what did a grateful country award him? A pension of 6d a day.

Albert's grandparents were able to live in two rooms of their own, because his grandmother was a midwife. Up to the age of eighty she was still delivering babies. Although she had absolutely no official qualifications for this job, it was her proud boast that in fifty years she could count the babies she had lost, on the fingers of one hand.

That families of twelve or more lived in such dire poverty, filth and squalor that many of the children didn't survive infancy—and perhaps they were better off not doing so—was nothing to do with the delivering of them. Most working-class families lost children, though not through lack of love. It was poverty and ignorance.

The highlight of his grandmother's life had been the day she visited the Great Exhibition in Hyde Park. She had never forgotten all the wonders and marvels, and was firmly of the opinion that there never could, or would, be another such event to equal it.

'Albert,' I asked, 'didn't you get bored with two such people? One living the past with his old comrades, and the other's conversation about babies and the Exhibition?'

'No I didn't. I liked being there. My grandfather counted as somebody. When he died he was given a military funeral. Besides, I was the only child. It was so different from being home with five sisters and two brothers. They let me do as I liked so long as I came in to meals. I was somebody there, I was important: Albert, their grandson. They never asked awkward questions, like: "have you washed your face, why are your boots dirty, how did you get on at school?". Anyway, it wasn't just my grandparents. My Aunt Rose and Uncle Sam lived there too; they quarrelled all the time. Aunt Rose worked at the R.S.A.

factory. She really was emancipated. She smoked like a chimney, chiefly Woodbines, liked drink, occasionally swore, and laughed at all the men who fancied her. Uncle Sam was in and out of jobs like a dog at a fair; he was a great disappointment to my grandfather. Nothing would have induced Uncle Sam to go into the army. Up to then his country had done nothing for him. Why should he leave a comfortable billet to be bawled at by sergeant-majors and have a pittance for a wage?'

Eventually, I discovered the real reason why Albert liked to go and stay with his grandparents. At the age of ten he fell headlong in love; not with some sugar-plum girl of his own age, no, with a friend of his Aunt Rose. Lizzie Thorne was about thirty to thirty-five. A very handsome lady with jet black hair, though not so well endowed in the bosom as his Aunt Rose. Albert caught them measuring themselves on one occasion. Lizzie Thorne's brother was the MP for Birmingham.

'It couldn't have been love, not at ten years old.'

'Well, if it wasn't, it was the most painful experience of my life. I have never felt the same emotion since. Aunt Rose knew at once how I felt. She would tease me by constantly bringing up Lizzie's name—I even thought the name, Lizzie, was a lovely name. By forever hanging around when she and Aunt Rose were together, by haunting the vicinity of the house where she lived, I finally got an invitation to tea. I nearly fainted with excitement on the day. I washed myself all over—and I can tell you that was a phenomenon as I wasn't much addicted to soap and water—I used some of Uncle Sam's evil-smelling violet oil on my hair, and polished my boots as though I was going on parade. And then, the worst thunderstorm of all time started. Peal upon peal of deafening thunder, continual forked-lightning, rain in torrents. My grandmother told me I couldn't possibly go to Lizzie's; that she would understand. I thought that my grandmother had gone mad. What, not go to tea? It would have taken an earthquake to keep me away. I ran through the streets, dodging falling tiles and chimney pots, drenched with rain, but with my ardour by no means quenched. And what a time I had. My fair lady—except that she was dark—fussed over me, gave me a towel to rub my hair and talked to me as though I was a grown-up. I nearly burst with emotion. The funny thing was that none of this affected my appetite. I gorged my way through bread and jam, pikelets, scones, sandwiches and cake; all the time gazing at her like a love-sick cow—or bull. After tea, she put records on the gramophone and let me wind it up, and we sang old music-hall ditties. When I was invited to stay for supper as well, I knew that life couldn't ever hold a greater joy. Even though the supper was tripe and onions, both of which I loathed in the normal way, because *she* had cooked it, it tasted like no tripe that ever was.'

Well, after that long recital from Albert, I looked at him with new eyes, I can tell you.

There was one place with which Albert never fell in love, and that was school, not to mention the teachers. He cordially disliked both. I imagine the feeling was mutual as Albert often played truant. His school, like mine, was never built for the comfort of the pupils. Dirty wooden floors, and desks obviously made by somebody who hadn't the remotest idea about the human anatomy in a sitting position. In the winter, one small coal fire that merely served to accentuate the enormous areas of arctic conditions. Every desk had been engraved by past pupils, who, knowing full well they would never leave their mark on the world, had determined to leave it on something.

A row of twelve lavatories was meant for the use of some two hundred boys. These 'conveniences' had no roofs, and the doors had gaps top and bottom. Toilet paper was seldom to be found as most of the kids used it to make spit-balls to throw in the class. In any case, this commodity was almost unknown in their homes, newspaper making an adequate substitute. As Albert told me, these lavatories were not places in which one wished to linger, especially on a cold or wet day—apart from the fact that numerous boys suffering from internal problems were banging on the doors or hurling missiles over the top.

Nevertheless a surprising amount of graffiti were written on the once white-washed walls. Most of it was of the 'Jack loves Lucy', 'George is teacher's pet' variety. But one never-to-be-forgotten day, the school cleaner found written 'My Dad says "Old Faggots" is a B.F. and not fit to run an infants' school.'

Fang-Wu, as the cleaner was called, on account of his one

solitary black tooth, loathed with a bitter hatred all the tribe of young manhood. He promptly informed the head teacher, Old Faggots. The whole school had to assemble in the hall to smoke out the culprit. Albert and his pal knew only too well who it was who had perpetrated this injustice on their 'beloved' head. After explaining the gravity of the offence, the disrespect to one set in authority over all, their head called for 'that boy' to come to the platform.

'Otherwise,' said Faggots, 'Friday football will be cancelled, and lessons substituted.'

'And did he succeed in finding out "who done it"?'

'Not on your life. What a hope. Who was going to own up and get a thrashing? First of all Old Faggots appealed to the better nature of the boy—we knew he didn't have one. Then he pointed out how all the school would suffer for one boy. But there were no Tom Browns in our school. Eventually, we got no football.'

'How noble of you not to split on the culprit,' I told Albert.

'Noble, my eye. Ernie Parker was much bigger than me, with fists of iron. I'd have told on him like a shot otherwise; anything to get out of lessons.'

In my school we did have a playground, although parts of it were rough and full of holes. In the winter, when the holes were full of rain-water, we got drenched if we fell in. In the dry weather, our knees were pitted as though some unknown plague had befallen us. But Albert's school was built with no provision for free time. They played cricket and football in the nearest park. At mid-morning break, the school being in a cul-de-sac, they played in the street—much to the fury of the nearby residents whose ears were assailed by shouts and catcalls, and whose gardens were ruined by hob-nailed boots searching for lost balls. 'Lots of the boys wandered off,' said Albert. 'Some to the nearest sweet shop, or to the baker's. There they could buy a halfpenny piece of Tottenham, which was a huge triangle of sponge cake oozing with jam. Or a halfpenny piece of kill-me-quick, which was a large square of fruit cake with the heaviness of lead. I generally went to the sweet shop and bought a halfpenny worth of mintshots. These were smaller than peas and one seemed to get over a hundred for a halfpenny. A favourite game in class was to suck them until the mint flavour was gone, and then shoot them at the other boys. I got so expert at this that once I shot one right into the inkwell on the master's desk—it was red ink too. With unconcealed glee the boys watched me go out to the front of the class. But apart from making me clean up the mess, the master, Old Hoppy, did nothing. I liked Old Hoppy, so called because he was so short that when he was caning anyone, he would jump in the air, to bring the ruler down with greater effect. The only time he used to cane me was on the occasions when I decided that it wasn't worth going back to school after the mid-morning break. I'd wander off to the park or canal, with a penny packet of five Woodbines to smoke, where nobody could find me. Even at twelve years old I couldn't resist a cigarette.

'Poor Old Hoppy,' said Albert, 'he hadn't a hope in heaven of getting through to us mob. The trouble with Hoppy was, he was convinced he understood boys; that by sweet reason and treating them as grown-ups, he could establish a kind of rapport.

'Unfortunately,' Albert explained, 'we weren't grown-up and had never heard of reason. We were mostly budding delinquents where education was concerned. Still, I liked Old Hoppy. In fact the only master I really hated was a Mr Matthews. He looked, and I'm sure was, obscene. He never caned boys on the hand. They had to bend over a chair. When they did this there was an expression of joy on the face of Mr Matthews. Only once was I called out, and I was fully determined to throw the chair at him if he told me to bend over—and then run for my life. I think he sensed this and I only got caned on the hand.'

Albert was never very enthusiastic about sport. Cricket wasn't too bad, but football, which generally degenerated into a free-for-all by the losing side, was something to be avoided if possible. 'I was never in the first or second eleven; I was never even sure what side I was on. Reserve for the third eleven I think. In fact,' said Albert, 'I was so seldom wanted that I often disappeared and nobody noticed. I think my position on the field was "left outside".'

In comparing our schooldays, Albert and I agree that the mass assembling for morning prayers and a hymn seemed a totally unnecessary event; something that one expected on Sundays only.

I was nearly always late for this as my Mother insisted that I did the shopping before I went to school, heedless of my protests that I would get into trouble for being late.

'You just tell your teacher that I can look after you better than the Almighty; after all, I know more about you. Tell her I'll say a prayer for you if she thinks it matters if you miss the school one.'

My Mum was not in favour of moral benefits. Except when they removed us all to school on a Sunday afternoon.

But nobody could have been more against religion than my friend Ursula's Mother. Ursula was the only girl in the school with such a name. All the girls tried to get her for a friend. Why she chose me that particular year I never knew. Already at eleven years, Ursula was bursting out all over with incipient womanhood; and unlike most of us who were confined in 'liberty bodices', Ursula was as free as air. She always appeared absolutely oblivious to her surroundings, be they school or home. Our teacher of that year let her get away with such unheard-of opinions that we were struck dumb. Like the morning she stood up in class saying, 'Excuse me, teacher. I shall be late in the mornings. My Mother says I am to miss hall assembly. She doesn't want my head stuffed up with all that Jesus rubbish.'

We sat open-mouthed at such temerity, sure that if teacher didn't strike her down, the Almighty would. But no. Ursula sat down unharmed. Mind you, most of us, ill-clad, cold and nearly always hungry, could not discern the blessings from above that were said to be showered upon us. Too well could we see in our daily life that 'to every one that hath shall be given'. We were far more concerned and involved in the struggle to retain even that which we had. Too often it was taken away.

That year when Ursula was my friend will never be forgotten by me. The highlight of each week was when I went to her house for tea. I liked Ursula's Mother, so different from mine. A huge shapeless woman whose physical protuberances, and mental exuberance, overflowed in all directions. She talked to us as though we knew all about life at eleven years old. Perhaps Ursula did.

'You know, girls,' her Mother would declare, 'I believe in mutual property. That we share and share alike.' Certainly, if rumour could be believed, she shared her ample charms on a fairly wide basis. I was fascinated by her personality and even more by the outward displays of affection, something that we never indulged in at home. Ursula's Mother would envelop me on leaving in an enormous embrace. I felt as though I would suffocate in the superfluous flesh.

'Sit down, my love,' she'd tell me, 'this is Liberty Hall. We believe in sharing.'

Certainly she shared her food with the mice that infested the house, and her beds with innumerable fleas. Poor Ursula sometimes came to school more spotted than a Dalmatian. Often, Ursula and I retired to her bedroom for long earnest discussions on life and its purpose. Then I would carry home some of the 'hoppers', much to the fury of my Mother. The extermination of these insects was her life-long task. Poor Mother; Dad worked in so many filthy houses that he often brought home enough fleas to supply every known circus.

When I look back at the amount of pests that infested our houses: mice, flies, bugs and fleas, it's a wonder we all kept so healthy. Probably we were exposed to so many germs that we became immune. Not that any family was unduly worried about this collection of fauna, looking upon them as part of life's rich pattern, or as 'Living with Nature'. I think that the mice were the worst plague; having a cat was the only way to keep them down. One place where we lived was overrun with these pests, but the landlady, who lived in the top half of the house, wouldn't allow us to have pets—and that included a cat. So we used to entice in any stray we found and keep it a few days, with the excuse that we were trying to find the owner. The only pets that old harridan would let us have were mice. These she provided in abundance, and for free. Mother used to lament, 'If only a Pied Piper would call here. He'd have more mice follow him than ever he had rats in Hamelin.'

One of the qualities that Ursula lacked was brains. This caused her no worry as her Mum was always saying, 'A head stuffed full of brains, means a stomach stuffed full of wind.' This piece of philosophy emanated from her experience with the late, but far from lamented, Mr Hill, the father of Ursula and her brother

Bartholomew—what a name to give a working-class boy. Incidentally, I detested him. He was fifteen and already working as an errand boy at the Maypole shop. A weedy, spotty youth addicted to pawing girls. He once tried to kiss me and it was simply revolting—enough to put me off for life.

Mr Hill wasn't 'late' in the sense that he had departed this life. He had merely departed from Mrs Hill's life. I must admit she seemed to bear him no malice for his lack of appreciation of home and family. 'You know, Margaret,' she told me—and I was delighted to be the recipient of this family saga—'it was his bloody parents that ruined our marriage. They were always telling him he had married below his station. His parents kept a shop while my old man was only a cobbler. They kept their Julian at school until he was sixteen and then got him a job in an office. When he was eighteen he met me at a dance—I was a pretty girl in those days, the boys hung round me like bees round a honey-pot.'

Mrs Hill could never have had a more appreciative listener than me. I was flattered, for I just couldn't imagine my Mother and me having confidential discussions about her past life.

'Go on, Mrs Hill,' I would urge her, 'what happened next?'

'What happened next, my dear, was that their bloody Julian got me in the family way.' And here she would burst out into an enormous bellow of laughter. 'Mind you, gal, I had to do most of the bloody work; he hadn't a clue.' I hadn't either, but I didn't tell her so.

'I'll never forget his Mother's face when we told her the news. Talk about a bloody lady. She screeched at me, "You're nothing but a whore. You led my son astray. He'll never marry you." I can tell you Margaret, it was "my son this" and "my son that", and all the time poor bloody Julian sat never saying a word.'

'Go on, Mrs Hill, what happened after that?'

Here she laughed so much that her very ample bosom and double chins undulated in unison. 'What happened? All hell! My Mum was up that house like a flash.'

'Like an avenging angel,' I interposed, momentarily disconcerting Mrs Hill, who obviously had never thought of her Mum in that role.

'If you say so, gal. She gave that woman a mouthful, I can tell you. Four-letter words showered on her like hail drops. "If my daughter wants to marry your son, she's bloody-well going to. Your precious Julian ruined her. My daughter's not the Virgin Mary, and your miserable son ain't Joseph. And when the brat arrives it's going to have a father, if my gal wants it to have one." So we got married and I got Bartholomew in wedlock.'

My opinion of that specimen was that he wasn't worth getting married for. When I asked Mrs Hill if she was sorry to have married Mr Hill, in view of his departure which left her with two kids, she quite cheerfully said, 'Poor blighter, he couldn't help being what he was with a Mother like that. She ruined him; made him too high and mighty for an ordinary job, and he wasn't clever enough to keep an office one. Oh! he had brains, but he never knew what to do with them. I was always saying to him, "your head stuffed full of brains, means our stomachs stuffed full of wind". I wasn't sorry when he cleared off. I've managed; I got friends.'

If my Mother had known that Ursula's Mum was relating all this family life to me, she would have been horrified. Mother believed that the longer children were kept in ignorance of the sordid side of life—and that definitely included a knowledge of sex—the better. In our house babies arrived unheralded, though certainly not unwanted. Mother has since told me that she did all she could to prevent too frequent births by way of quinine, pennyroyal and gin—the latter to be preferred—but when nothing worked, well, another infant arrived.

Ursula's lack of brains meant that we separated during school hours. Our teacher, acting on the assumption that the bright girls—this included me—would work without constant supervision, put us in the back row of the class. The dunces sat in the front. If only Ursula could have sat next to me I would have let her copy my work. No public-school code prevailed in our class; everyone who needed to cheat, and could do so without being caught, did so without any feeling of doing wrong. Only a few of us really liked school. The others looked upon teachers as natural enemies, and school as a place where they had to serve 'ten years hard'. Once, in class, I sent Ursula, via the intervening rows, all the answers to our general knowledge test. Unfortunately, our lynx-eyed Miss Goddard saw this sleight-of-hand with disastrous results for me.

But it was when we came out of school that Ursula reigned supreme. With her well-developed bosom, fair hair and blue eyes, she had dozens of boys hanging around her all the way home. Me they took very little notice of, except inasmuch as I was Ursula's friend and might put in a good word for them. In any case, I wasn't interested in boys just then, for I had suddenly become emotionally involved with our teacher, Miss Goddard, though I don't think she ever knew.

One of the school subjects at which I didn't excel was drawing; in fact I hadn't the faintest idea of lines, or perspectives. Miss Goddard used to sit down next to me, to try and help me to overcome this disability. If only she had known what pure unalloyed joy it was to have her so near; so many emotions and feelings went through me that I often felt like fainting with bliss. Far from improving in art, I made sure that I got worse, just to have the pleasure of Miss Goddard's proximity.

Ursula and I used to discuss this passion of mine in the privacy of her bedroom, until she began to get bored with my constant soul-searchings. Probably we would have drifted apart gradually, but the process was accelerated by my Mother. The fleas she put up with, but when it came to finding my hair infested, my Mother flatly forbade me to go to Ursula's house again. I appealed to my Father, but in vain. Although I was his favourite child and he was very indulgent towards me, Father was always one for a quiet life, and my Mother generally over-ruled him. I was in a terrible state about this. I felt that she had ruined my life and had done permanent damage to my character. Perhaps she had. But in those days, very few parents bothered about the opinions of their children, and such persons as psychologists and psychiatrists were unheard of. Probably we were none the worse for their absence.

Although my parents were in love with each other all their lives—they had been married nearly fifty years when my Father died—I felt then that my Father would have been a happier man if my Mother had not been such a dominant woman. But I think differently now. I think that they complemented each other. That my Father needed a dominant woman to justify his own far from go-ahead and aggressive nature. That he could feel, 'I need to be like I am, to keep my wife happy and in love. If I assert myself it will cause discord.'

Albert and I have very different natures. He is an introvert. But as he never minds what I do, he makes a super husband. Because Albert had, and still has, a very independent and self-sufficient nature, he had no special friends at school; he says that he has never needed friends in the sense that life was incomplete without them. Unlike me, he is not naturally gregarious, preferring the company of his family to that of outsiders.

Albert's schooldays seemed to have made very little impression on him, judging by the few incidents he can recall. 'I was just an average boy, and that's all I ever wanted to be. Average boys have the best time. They are not expected to be brilliant at any particular subject. I have only two recollections of any claim to fame at school. The first one was at one of our painting lessons. I was colouring a sketch of a bowl of apples. When I had finished, our teacher held my drawing up to the class, saying, "These apples look real enough to eat." I went brick-red with surprise and gratification. For sure, I thought, this masterpiece will adorn the classroom wall—I had never had one there before. But when this effort of mine joined most of the others in the waste paper basket, the worm of discontent so gnawed at me, that never again did I try to rise above the rank and file.'

'And what was your other claim to fame?'

'Oh! that was when I ruptured myself through trying to climb on to the roof of our headmaster's study. Nobody in our class could do it, but they all dared me to. Halfway up I fell down on to the concrete and had to be rushed to hospital. Although I was only ten years old, they put me with the men. Perhaps the children's ward was full. I had a lovely time there. One of the nurses, a pretty little girl called Betty, used to kiss me every morning—much to the fury of the man in the next bed to me. But then I was a model patient, while he was the bane of the nurses. Even now I laugh when I think of the morning he came in; a great hairy hunk of a man—he'd injured his leg on the docks. As his usual conversation was so peppered with swear words that even the nurses blushed, and they were used to rough customers, this man got none of the little extra attentions that the nurses, however hard-worked they were, usually gave to the patients.

'When the doctor came round and asked this Joe how he felt, Joe said, "Bloody awful, else I wouldn't be in this bloody place. Bloody row that goes on here's like being in Bedlam and this bed's as hard as my mother-in-law's heart." I thought him very funny but nobody else seemed to. But even the other patients admired his pluck when the specialist paid his weekly visit. This awesome person came into the ward like some visiting royalty, flanked by the house-surgeon, the sister, staff nurse and several ordinary nurses. We were too dead scared to speak when he stopped by our beds. But not Joe. Very few of these eminent experts ever spoke a word to the patients they examined, and this one seemed extra contemptuous of their feelings. So after looking at Joe's leg, he went into a confab with the house-surgeon. Suddenly Joe electrified the ward by saying, "Here you, expert, or whatever you call yourself. If you've got anything to say about my leg, say it to me. It's my bloody property. And you ain't taking it off, not if I have to crawl out of this hospital on my bloody knees." '

The specialist was so astounded that he actually called Joe Mr Green, and told him he wouldn't have to have his leg amputated.

'But surely, Albert,' I enquired, 'you must have found something of interest to do in school?'

'The only lesson that I liked was woodwork. But as this started only a year before I left school, I never had the opportunity to become proficient. Even in that short time I managed to make my Mother a teapot-stand and my Dad a pipe-holder. The fact that my Mother kept the teapot permanently on the hob, and my Dad never smoked a pipe, was beside the point. I made them. I'm sure that if I could have had more lessons I'd have become an expert carpenter. As it is, I just knock nails in wood and generally mess around.'

Mess around is right, judging by Albert's efforts in this house.

The first thing he made, a three-legged stool for the bathroom, rapidly became a two-legged stool after I sat on it. My wrath was not appeased by Albert saying that I must have sat on the edge of the stool. His second effort was a picture frame. 'I'm using dowel pins for this,' he informed me. I hadn't a clue what a dowel pin was. I only knew that the frame hadn't been on the wall a week before the bottom fell out and the glass too.

'Can't understand what happened,' said Albert. 'I followed the instructions to the letter.'

'Don't bother to make any more frames, let's buy them. It will be cheaper in the long run than having to keep buying glass. Obviously some people can dowel, and some can't,' I explained very nicely to Albert.

Unfortunately, nothing seems to dampen that man's enthusiasm for do-it-yourself. Those experts on radio and television, who are forever talking and showing how easy it all is, have a lot to answer for. I wouldn't mind betting that they have ruined some erstwhile harmonious marriages. Nothing is more conducive to the ruination of a happy home than for the wife to be continually surrounded by, and falling over, all the paraphernalia of these do-it-yourself maniacs. As fast as they have finished one project, they start on something else.

Albert's latest *objet d'art* is a record cabinet; and I can tell you, to my eye at any rate, it's very far from being a thing of beauty and a joy for ever. In fact, if the doors were removed and a piece of wire netting nailed across, it would make a very good rabbit hutch. I wanted to buy a cabinet, but no, 'anyone can knock up a simple piece like that', Albert assured me. Knock up is the operative word. Still, I don't really mind. Albert is very good at odd jobs around the house. I tried to get him to join the evening class for carpentry, but he refused to go back to school. Can't bear to be reminded of the days of his youth. Albert reckoned that the best way to survive the rigours of school life was to become as inconspicuous as possible, dodging praise and blame with equal facility. What a way to spend ten formative years of one's life! I never felt like that; I liked school and most of the lessons. But not biology, or as it was called then, nature lesson. Unlike the explicit teaching in schools today about the art, or act, of procreation, our lessons on the subject were so wrapped in a cocoon of proprietry as to obscure completely their true meaning.

When we were taught about the mating habits of the birds and the bees, they were just that, and no more. Even to know that the queen bee was pursued by dozens of male bees longing to fertilise her, never made us correlate this with human relationships. Most working-class parents' ambition was to be respectable, and this state definitely excluded even the word 'sex'. In my home, in spite of over-crowding, none of us, after the age of five or six, ever slept in our parents' room. If we heard sounds of upheaval from their room, we attributed it to sleeplessness—or just things that went bump in the night.

Chapter 2

When Albert was born, his Father was a slater's labourer, but by the time he was four years old, his Father had become a baker. How the transition was effected Albert never knew. On the face of it there seems no connection between the two jobs. Presumably, a slater's labourer has to run up and down a ladder with the slates for the slater on the roof. As Albert's Father was perhaps too fond of his beer, he may have found running up and down a ladder carrying a pile of slates a rather hazardous proceeding. Especially as alcohol, far from inducing a feeling of bonhomie, made him even more choleric. Not that the heat of the bakehouse improved his temper, and the other men took care not to upset him when he was using the peel.

Albert was twelve years old when the First World War started. As he had two older brothers, the war was always under discussion in his home; mostly with excitement by his brothers, who wished that they were old enough to go. At that time most people thought the war would be over in six months.

My Mother loathed war and was bitter in her denunciation of all those so-called patriots who welcomed it with chauvinistic ardour. When she read aloud the letters in the newspaper from retired colonels advocating immediate conscription, her rage was enough to have annihilated them. She couldn't understand why the public weren't horrified at the very thought of the senseless killings. Towards the end they were. But in the beginning the idea of vanquishing an enemy seems to give a spiritual uplift, like going on a crusade. It's when the horrors become known and death enters their home, that people's enthusiasm fades. There was no lack of ardent volunteers at the beginning of that war. As for the posters which appeared later on in the war, showing lurid pictures of alleged 'German swinishness', my Mother would have torn them down if possible. Not because she loved Germans, she had no feelings one way or the other, but because she thought such posters were a direct incitement to rouse all the worst in human nature. My Father could never understand why she got so worked up. For as long as possible he ignored the whole affair.

Other posters my Mother treated with derision. One read, 'Women of Britain say "Go",' which Mother dismissed as an absolute lie as none of the women she knew were voicing such sentiments. Another, 'Waste not, Want not', obviously didn't apply to us as we seldom had enough food, let alone a surplus. As for the prolific posters of little white-haired old ladies saying goodbye to their sons as they urged them into uniform, as Mother said, 'One would imagine some organic change had taken place, producing a generation of white-haired female dwarfs.'

Down in Hove I remember seeing only one or two Zeppelins, but Albert, living in London, saw many. For in 1915, when the Zeppelins first appeared, England had no defence against them at all. Nobody in authority seemed to have foreseen that our island security was at an end. They came over without a sound, the silvery-grey of the dirigible almost invisible against the clouds. We had no weapons capable of reaching them in the skies. This was the first time in history that the civilian population had experienced war from the air—and there were no air-raid shelters then. We were told at school that the Kaiser had produced this terrible weapon especially to exterminate the English, as he hated them. It does seem rather short-sighted to have produced a weapon as vulnerable as the Zeppelin proved to be. Nevertheless, the fear of these night-raiders appearing in our skies made the government order restrictions on lighting, though the result was only a dim-out compared with the black-out of the Second World War.

'It was some time in August 1915 when I first saw a Zeppelin over London,' said Albert. 'It was about midnight, and we heard people shouting in the street. We all rushed to the windows, but at first nothing could be seen. Then suddenly, in a gap in the clouds, loomed this incredibly graceful object. We were so fascinated that no thought of danger ever entered our heads. Later, the next day, we heard that the Zeppelin had dropped bombs on Leyton, killing ten people and wounding others. After that, my parents and the neighbours ceased to regard the airships solely as objects of beauty. It wasn't long before the newspapers printed dozens of letters from people who, tired of forever taking shelter in the Underground, wanted to know what the Government were doing, or going to do, about protecting the civilian population. Mr Balfour, like Churchill, merely reiterated his opinion that nothing would destroy the nerve of the British people.'

When I read this out to my Mother she said, 'Fine words. I wonder where *he* is when the bombs are falling on London? Somewhere safer than the Underground, I bet.'

'One of the worst air-raids,' Albert continued, 'took place later that year when at least five Zeppelins managed to get to London. Until Mother made us all get in the cupboard under the stairs, my brothers and I watched from our bedroom window. I remember how excited we got at seeing these sausage-shaped objects continually caught in the beams of the searchlights. But they were flying too high for our guns to reach them. My brothers and I were shouting out to the Germans to go home and yelling threats of what would be done to them if they got shot down. That night, bombs were dropped on the Strand; the Lyceum was hit, Kingsway and Gray's Inn. I believe about twenty or more people were killed. My two brothers got dressed and rushed off to look at the fires, but my Mother wouldn't let me go; said that she needed a man to protect the family as my Father wasn't there—he was working in the bakehouse at night.'

We had no such dramatic experiences in Hove, and I can't remember any bombs falling, even from the Zeppelin that came over at midnight on a Saturday. What I chiefly remember is the shock of seeing our ordinary friends and neighbours standing on the pavement in their night-attire—or rather lack of it. Such luxury as a dressing gown was unheard of. The women stood with old coats over their nightdresses. Some were too poor to own even a nightdress and obviously went to bed wearing their petticoats. But the men looked the funniest, standing there in vests and long-johns, for none of them owned a pair of pyjamas.

At night they undressed as far as their underwear and got into bed—at least it didn't take long to get off to work in the morning. After a day of long hours of hard work, few men cared about the idea of being attractive in bed, or bothered about the preliminaries. You got your husband smelling of good honest sweat—well, sweat anyway. At least you knew you had a man in bed with you. Nowadays, what with men's silk pyjamas, aftershave lotions, deodorants, bath-salts, and the long hair, a woman could be excused for wondering who the hell's sharing her bed.

By 1916 Albert's oldest brother was eighteen and was immediately called-up for war service. He contracted consumption through the continuous cold and wet in the trenches and died when he was only thirty-five. By this time too, the Government had set up the Tribunals before which conscientious objectors had to appear. According to my Mother, these Tribunals were presided over by a collection of old men just out of mothballs, long past the exercise of any of their vital functions but capable of breathing fire and slaughter over any man who had a conscientious objection to killing humans. My Father, the kindest and mildest of men, would never go before one of these Tribunals. Amid the mounting fanaticism and fury of war, the effort required to become a conscientious objector was beyond his powers. It was easier to be called-up. Mother, frantic at the thought of losing her beloved Harry—we children were no substitute for him—continually went on at Dad. 'Your country has never done anything for you but let you starve when you had no work and half-kill yourself for a pittance of wages when you had. And, mark my words, your country will do nothing for you when this war is over. The only ones who stand to gain are the politicians and armament manufacturers.'

As for actually volunteering to fight, 'madness!' Mother couldn't understand that men went to war for a variety of reasons, of which love of their country was only one. Boredom, the search for adventure and excitement, a chance to become somebody, all these facets of life played a part.

When eventually my Father was conscripted in 1916, the medical board graded him C.3., and my Mother's fears for her loss and Dad's safety were allayed. But the desperate shortage of men soon resulted in Dad being called-up and sent to France.

'I would have been about fourteen then,' said Albert, 'and had just left school. My departure from that scene occasioned no show of interest from the masters, and certainly no grief for me. In fact my nine and a half years there made very little impression on my life. Not that I knew what to do with my freedom. I hadn't the slightest idea what sort of a job I wanted. And our school had never heard of a careers master. Our life ended at fourteen as far as they were concerned. They probably assumed that such a motley collection of misfits weren't likely to have anything as grand as a "career"; and our ambition was just to finish being incarcerated for about six hours every day.'

'But didn't you have any ideas on what you were going to do with your life? After all—you'd got a lot of it to look forward to.'

'I wanted to get into the War. As I was too young, I got a job with a dairy, pushing a milk-barrow around the streets. I felt really somebody: my own milk-round at fourteen. Unfortunately my importance was somewhat deflated by not being able to see over the top of the barrow. After knocking over two bikes left leaning against the kerb, and almost flattening a dog, I was reduced to peering out from side to side as I pushed my barrow.

'The previous owner of the round, before he went into the Army, had alerted me to all the tricks of the trade: the milkman's perks. The dented-in milk cans, the legerdemain needed to pour out from a half-pint measure into a jug, always leaving a residue of milk in the measure, and to tot up the weekly accounts so swiftly that you bewildered the housewife into not noticing how she had paid for a pint she hadn't had—no computer could have been quicker than I.'

'But surely, Albert, all these reprehensible practices were hardly what a young and innocent fourteen-year-old should know about?'

'Young and innocent my eye. Nobody could live in our neighbourhood and remain so. Besides, old Bert, the previous milkman, had put the fear of the Lord into me, saying, "Boy, when I get out of this bloody army, I'll want my job back. And if you've ruined my takings by being bloody honest, I'll have the hide off your back." I really thought he could do it, too.' Well, that's Albert's story, and he's sticking to it.

Back in my home we were barely able to live on the Government's meagre separation allowance. So my eleven-and-a-half-year-old brother got a Saturday job as a lather boy in a barber's shop, while I, at nine years old, got a Saturday morning job lighting the fires for orthodox Jewish families. They weren't allowed to do this on their Sabbath, but as a 'goy' it was all right for me to do it. My brother worked very hard, from eight o'clock in the morning until eight o'clock at night. He got 3/6d—17½p today—for all those hours. As most working-class men had to work until one o'clock on a Saturday, the busiest time in the barber's shop was always the afternoon and early evening. This was the one day of the week on which the men bothered to shave. Then in the evening, dressed in his Sunday best, a man would go to the pub—while his wife followed about two hours later. Afterwards, in his home, fortified by the strong beer and the fact that he had worked only a half-day, the husband would indulge in what was crudely known as 'having a bit'. It's now known as 'having it off' or 'making love' and seems to require a great many variations on a theme. But not for the manual worker of those days. If they had ever heard of 'fifty-seven varieties', they and their wives—who had no home appliances to make housework easy—were too tired to bother. As for all the talk that one hears today on 'how to keep your marriage exciting', they would have hooted with derision at the idea. It probably wasn't very exciting even at the beginning.

I had to get up at the crack of dawn for my fire-lighting jobs, but I didn't mind. As well as the coppers that I earned, I nearly always got something to eat. It was very easy for me to look pathetic and gaze longingly at their food.

Early in 1918 Albert's family moved to Rochester, in Kent. His Father's boss, who owned the bakery, had recently settled there and opened another bakehouse. As good dough-makers were as scarce as gold nuggets, he asked his best one, Albert's Father, if he would consider moving to Rochester with a higher wage.

'It was great at first,' Albert remembers. 'We had gone up in the world. From living in rooms in London we now had a house, with our own front door. We actually could have a front room, "holy of holies". All we needed to complete it was a piano with an aspidistra on top. But we never managed to attain those luxuries—not that any of us could have played the piano. Naturally, the house had no bathroom or inside lavatory. But it did have a garden at the back; a real garden, with real earth, not just a concrete yard; a garden where my Mother, in her mind's eye, saw rows of potatoes and peas; a garden which our cat could use instead of having to have a box indoors. Unfortunately, on these open-air expeditions, our cat seemed to want the company of his own kind, so various other cats made themselves little holes in our garden. We might just as well have harboured moles. Such was the back-breaking task of digging that "good earth" that the enthusiasm, on us kids' part at any rate, rapidly declined. By the time we had removed the rubble and dug up two rusty bike-frames, dozens of old tyres, portions of a bed-frame and an old kitchen fender, even my Father gave up. "Let's not bother about growing things, let's just keep chickens and rabbits. It will be much less work." But my Mother was a determined woman. She needed to be with eight children and a somewhat erratic husband. She made that garden grow. It wasn't exactly like the Garden of Eden, but at least it did produce something.'

Soon after this, Albert's brother Redvers wanted to enlist in the army because his best pal was going. As Redvers was only seventeen-and-a-half he had to get his parents' permission, which they very reluctantly gave. Redvers hadn't been in France six months before his leg got blown off and his pal blown to pieces right next to him. And as the war went on and on, Albert's parents began to get worried that he too would become a victim of the insatiable call for men. So Albert's Father got him a job in the bakehouse, a reserved occupation.

'I only lasted two weeks,' said Albert. 'At that time the dough was kneaded by hand, and my Father was expert at getting the right mixture and temperature. But I couldn't stick it. What with the volcanic heat of the bakehouse and all that dough punching, I was as limp as a wet rag. Next I got a job as an apprentice in Aveling & Porter; they made tools. I started as a bot-turner, and it would have been a good job if I could have stayed there. But the noise of the machines was enough to drive one mad. All day long the racket never ceased. Even at night I heard it in my sleep. One day, after I had been there a few months, I had an epileptic attack. So that was the end of that job and back to being a milk roundsman again.

'But living down there soon began to bore me. I found that I missed London: the life in the streets, the parks and canals. Besides, being a stranger in Rochester and Chatham, one felt an outcast. So many families had intermarried, and formed a tight clan because so many worked on the docks. But at least we couldn't be accused of leaving London to avoid the air-raids. On every clear night they would come over the Kent coast on their way to London; at least, they must have hoped that it was the route to London although some of the Zeppelins found themselves anywhere but. On the way back, if they hadn't been able to drop their bombs, they let them go before they crossed the Channel; surprisingly little real damage was done.'

When the First World War was over, it seemed as though life got back to normal with remarkable rapidity. Albert's parents were thankful that their two sons were safely home, even although one had lost his leg. They didn't know then that their eldest son would die of consumption because of his war service.

My Mother was thankful, not only because she hated the war, but because she had now justified her previous opinions. 'You see,' my Mother would tell Dad, 'I told you all along that the Government appeals to patriotism and sacrifice, their recognition of our existence, would all fade out once they didn't need us. We could all be dead now for all it matters to them.' I must admit that our financial position seemed just as precarious. But Mother admits now that there was a change. The gradual emancipation of women, both politically and in the opportunity and ability to enter a man's world, the growth of trade unionism, and above all the changes in dress, all these came about, if not wholly as a result, certainly as part of the aftermath of war. And I'm sure that we were never quite so hard-up as we had been. Dad seemed to get more work. If only he hadn't been addicted to his little flutter on the horses. In spite of his kind and easy-going nature,

Mum could never cure him of his gambling, of his dreams of making 'real money'. But why shouldn't he dream? For a man of my Father's nature a brief sojourn in a fantasy world was a necessity. It enabled him to face the grim realities. Besides, Dad only wanted the money for Mum and us. Poor Dad. I can see him now on a Saturday dinner time facing our Mum with an already depleted pay packet—he'd had a bet.

'But Flo,' Dad would try to placate her, 'it's an absolute cert to romp home. I put the bet on with old Bill and his sister's nephew works as a stablehand where the horse is trained.'

Mum would not be appeased. She knew only too well, from past experience of Dad's certs, that the horse would not only not romp home, but would probably still be running after the others were in their stalls. My heart ached for Dad but I didn't dare interfere; I feared my Mother too much. At the same time I couldn't really blame Mother for her wrath. The struggle to keep a roof over our heads, to get clothes of a sort to wear, and enough food, took all her time and ingenuity. She did love Dad, although his lack of will-power irritated her. Everybody loved my Father, but Mum has since told me he loved me the most.

When things had settled down to normal, Dad resumed his old Sunday morning habit of visiting his relatives—he wouldn't go within a mile of Mum's—while Mother cooked the Sunday dinner. I always went with him, and any other of my brothers or sisters who wanted to come. We'd call on our grandparents, aunts, uncles and cousins. Now I look back on those occasions I feel that we weren't always welcomed with unconcealed joy. Probably they would have preferred to have Dad without us. Especially as we generally sat there listening to every word, ready to retell it to Mother when we got back home. And we found that it paid off to be all ears. We generally got a penny to get us out of the house and round to the sweet shop. I seldom got bored with these outings, for not only did I enjoy being with my Dad, I also liked listening to grown-up conversation. Mother didn't mind Dad going out with us. But later, when we got too old, and Dad took to going on his own, Mum suddenly found it more convenient to have the Sunday dinner on a Saturday, leaving her free.

Chapter 3

Albert was eighteen when he decided to leave Rochester. His departure was accelerated by the decision of his boss, who found that employing Albert on a milk-round was more of a liability than an asset.

'My misfortunes were never wholly my fault,' Albert told me—well they never are, are they?

'I could never see eye to eye with the foreman. He was one of the most disagreeable and meanest-tempered men I have met.'

'That's exactly how I feel about people who don't see my point of view. And what were all your misfortunes?'

'Well, doing a milk-round in those days wasn't a piece of cake as it is now, when nearly all milkmen deliver by mechanical power. I had to be on the round at four a.m. and in the winter it was so cold that the top of the milk churn used to freeze, and I couldn't pour the milk. So I used to take a pile of newspapers with me, and every now and then I would light one and hold it under the tap to thaw it out. No easy job. You want to try it in the early hours, perished with the cold. One morning the damn tap wouldn't thaw, so in a rage I lit a whole pile of newspapers under it. It wasn't my fault that the whole lot flared up and burnt the paint off the milk-barrow, though I do admit it was unfortunate that it was a new one my boss had just bought. Then there was the day of the "great exposure".'

'What on earth was that? Something to do with pornography?'

'Certainly not. Part of my round was to deliver milk to a row of almshouses, in a sort of Close. I would lift up their kitchen windows, take the little jugs they had put there ready, and leave a half-pint of milk in them. One morning, in a fit of abstraction, I opened the communal bathroom windows, a mistake anybody could make. There were two of the old dears inside, stark naked.

The screechings could have been heard in the next town, you'd have thought I was climbing through to assault them. I've never shut a window so quickly in my life. A complaint was made and my boss was furious. But as I told him, if I had wanted to see females in the nude it wouldn't be two old dears from the almshouses. He accepted my explanation over this, but maybe it was a bit too much when I lost the milk-barrow the following week.'

'What do you mean, "lost it"? How could you lose a milk-barrow?'

'I don't mean permanently lost it. One morning while I was down in a basement leaving cans of milk, the barrow ran down the hill into the High Street. At the bottom it over-turned and two gallons of milk poured out down the road. All the cats in creation were out like a flash, they'd never had such a bun-day. But did my boss appreciate this kindness to dumb animals? He did not.'

'Was that when you got the sack?'

'Oh no! I got the sack at Christmas. On Christmas Eve I, and the other three roundsmen, finished work in a distinctly merry mood; at nearly every house, we were offered tots of whisky or gin. I remember that I pushed my barrow back to the yard as though it weighed no more than a puff of wind. At that time, when we had finished our rounds, we had to wash out our own cans and churns, and hard work it was. For months the boss had been promising to employ a man just to do this washing up. But nothing had come of it. So on this day, big-like, I said to the men, I'm going to tackle that blighter of a foreman about a washer-up. Why should we keep doing it and not get any more money.

' "That's right, Bert, you do it. Go on, have a go at him", they urged me. So I marched up to the foreman's office, with them a safe distance behind, and told him in no uncertain terms that either he got a washer-up or I got my cards. My bold front collapsed like a punctured balloon when he just went into the office and handed me my cards. My three supporters by this time had melted away like snow in summer. I appealed to our boss; but as the foreman had worked for him for ten years and I only two, it was me who had to go.'

33

When Albert went back to London at eighteen, I had just left school at thirteen, to the sorrow of our headteacher who told my parents that I would have made a good teacher if they could have afforded to leave me at school. I didn't shed any tears, or leave with a chip on my shoulder, as I'd known for a long time that my parents needed any money I could earn. I felt a little sad at saying goodbye to dear Miss Goddard—though I had long got over the 'pash' I had had on her. She did invite me to come and see her at her home and I fully intended to do so then, but somehow the idea of talking to her when I was no longer a school-girl seemed incongruous, so I never went. I very soon got a job. There was no lack of daily work for a big, strong girl. For my first job, working from 9.00 a.m. until 1.00 p.m., seven days a week, breakfast but no mid-day meal, I got 10/-. That worked out at about 3d per hour—or 1½p.

Albert got himself a furnished room, and a job with a butcher, in Church Street, Kensington.

'After a lot of arguing with the boss, I managed to get £2 a week as wages, plus a weekly joint. He wanted to pay me only 30/-, the same as the other two assistants got. "Don't tell them what you're getting," he admonished me, "or they will be asking for a rise." I believe we were all earning the same wage. That crafty man just wanted me to think I was favoured.'

After Albert had been in London about six months, his Father joined him. His Father's temper, uncertain at the best of times, had become increasingly choleric during the last few months; so much so, that the other workers in the bakehouse threatened to walk out if he didn't go. Probably the heat of working under-ground, in a sweltering atmosphere, wasn't conducive to harmony; anyway his ire rose quicker than the bread did. I wondered how Albert and his Father managed with only one room and one single bed.

'That was no problem,' Albert explained. 'My Father soon got another baker's job. When I went off to work in the morning, he had just finished work, so the bed was never empty. It wasn't a very hygienic way of living but we couldn't worry about the niceties. I wasn't too happy about him living with me. I didn't much care for my Father, principally because of the way he treated Mother, and my Father seemed to dislike me. We lived in a kind of neutrality, until the day he tried to please me by making a rice pudding—he knew I liked this. But not having any idea how to make it, apart from the fact that it needed milk, rice and sugar, he used about half a pound of rice. The resulting dish was as solid as the Rock of Gibraltar. Even then all might have passed over if my Father hadn't been drinking whisky instead of beer. When he saw me trying to get a fork in this solid mass, and laughing, he got up to hit me. I put up my fists and knocked him back on the chair. That was the last time my Father tried anything on me. In any case, my Mother soon came back to London, and we got rooms again. There weren't so many of us now. My two oldest sisters and brother were married, and Redvers soon cleared out—he had a war pension to live on. The next person to clear out was my Father. He had already indulged in spasmodic vanishing tricks, but always rematerialised within a few days. This time his departure was permanent. As the only son left at home, my Mother depended on me and we became even more attached to each other. At least I was reliable and came home every evening.'

I didn't realise how deeply attached Albert was to his Mother until we got married, when he would still call in to see her at least three times a week. At that time, not knowing all the circumstances, I thought such devotion excessive. It lessened the amount that I got.

'I stayed five years at that butcher's,' said Albert, 'a record for me at that time. At first I rode a bicycle around, calling at the basements of the big houses to get the orders from the cooks. I really enjoyed that because more often than not I was asked into the kitchen and made a fuss of. Most of the servants seemed to like me.'

'Ah well! they naturally would. And,' I added, deflating Albert's ego, 'servants saw so few of the opposite sex that almost anything in trousers and capable of functioning as a man was an event.'

'It wasn't like that at all,' Albert protested vehemently. 'Not all my customers were easy-going. One cook was so sour and severe that she used to terrify me. As for the pathetic little kitchenmaid, Martha, she hardly dared give me the time of day before that old harridan jumped on her. This cook, Mrs Howard, informed me that she had worked for "real gentry". I'd no idea what she meant. To me, anybody who could afford to have servants was gentry. This Mrs Howard was about sixty, so she certainly had no hopes of ever getting married and leaving domestic service—maybe that's what made her so foul and bitchy to poor Martha. Some mornings this cook would take one look at the meat, and promptly tell me that Madam wouldn't eat such poor stuff. When I took it back to the shop, my boss would chop the corners off, flatten it with the side of the chopper, tie it up afresh, and I'd take it back again.

'"Ah," exclaimed the cook, "that's more like it, why couldn't you have brought it like that the first time?"'

It was through being a butcher that Albert lost a portion of himself, though not a vital portion fortunately. It all happened because he was enamoured of a pretty Irish cook called Molly— she was probably on the lookout for a husband and I bet, being the cook, she was at least ten years older than Albert; but she used to give him tea and hot scones, and on any pretext ring the shop for things she could easily have waited for until the next day—just to get Albert round there again. One thing I feel sure she didn't give him. She never made the ultimate sacrifice; very, very few servants did. As virginity was their only dowry, it had to be preserved for the right and legal occasion.

'I was very fond of Molly, she was very good to me. At Christmas, knowing my Mother's circumstances, Molly gave me a pudding and a cake for her. I couldn't resist telling them at work how popular I was, and then I had to listen to ribald remarks concerning "pudding clubs", and how mean it was not to share any of these treats. So one evening, I brought the pudding into the shop to share it out. For a joke, young Fred went to chop it in half with an old rusty chopper, with calamitous consequences, for he chopped off the top of my finger as well. I remember all four of us stood there dumbfounded; I hadn't felt a thing when it happened. Now I stared at this severed lump of flesh feeling very peculiar indeed.

'"Quick," said Bill, the oldest of us, "we must get Bert to a doctor before he gets lockjaw." Very cheerful person was Bill. So they wrapped my finger, and the severed stump, in a piece of cheese cloth and rushed me to the nearest doctor. He poured iodine over it—which nearly killed me as the feeling was coming back to me by then—and sent me to the hospital. As by now it was late evening, we had to sit for what seemed like hours in the casualty department. The waiting was enlivened by gruesome and vivid inner pictures of me dying from loss of blood or gangrene. When I finally saw the doctor he said far too much time had elapsed for the stump to be sewn on. It should have been done within minutes. So he just stitched the top of my finger. On the way back from the hospital, fortified by several glasses of strong ale, we discussed what to do with the stump of my finger—I was carrying it in my pocket. Many and lurid were the macabre and obscene suggestions. Suddenly, Bill said, "Why not give it to Molly as a souvenir? After all, indirectly the accident was her fault. Besides, she might like to sleep with it under her pillow. It will give her pleasant dreams of you." '

'Further gross and bawdy remarks followed about the object being a somewhat inadequate substitute for the real thing. Eventually, we chucked it into the Grand Union Canal.'

Gradually, as Albert became expert at this butcher's job, cutting up carcasses into joints and salting silversides and flanks, he began to get grandiloquent ideas of his future. He even visualised himself as a buyer at Smithfield, and becoming known as a 'sharp man, with an eye'. In Albert's imagination he had his own shop, in fact several shops scattered round London. But with all high-flown and high falutin' ideas, the actual realisation is a long and laborious process. It requires more than dreams. Practical application, sheer hard work and nose to the grindstone are the qualities necessary. None of these is exactly appealing. But Albert says the actual reason that he left the butcher's job was because he no longer went around on a bicycle calling on people, having become too useful in the shop. His boss was as sorry to lose him, as Albert's Mother was to lose the free supply of meat she had enjoyed for so long.

'But it was through working there and calling at houses that I met one of the best friends I have ever had. This was William

Green, second porter at a block of service flats. He was fourteen years older than me. We went everywhere together and I saw him nearly every single night for eleven years. That was when I met you, Margaret. But it wasn't until long afterwards that I realised what it must have meant to William when I broke away.'

Albert didn't understand at the time. I didn't either. With the crass egotism of youth and inexperience, I only saw and felt that William must be remarkably dense or insensitive if he thought that we wanted his frequent company so soon after our marriage. William suffered from a speech defect, which made it difficult to understand some of his words—though later on I was able to converse with him as though his speech was normal. He was the kindest of men; how we would have survived without him during the six months that Albert was out of work I don't know.

'My pal William and John, the third porter, had furnished bed-sitting rooms in the basement, with use of bathroom. Mr Palmer, the head porter, had a small flat, as did Molly Morgan the housekeeper. Oh! she fancied herself with the men, did Molly Morgan. Always rolling her black eyes at them. Even the way she walked was an open invitation to follow her. All the policemen on the beat knew Molly Morgan. The men even hummed a ribald ditty about her that rhymed with "organ".

'Needless to say,' added Albert, 'she didn't bother to be sexy with small fry such as William and me. But William knew that she and the head porter were having an affair—I suppose it would be called "having it off" nowadays—for he'd seen Mr Palmer leaving her room in the middle of the night.' What was William doing out of *his* room in the middle of the night?

'Personally, neither William nor I would have had anything to do with a woman like Molly Morgan, even if she had handed it to us on a plate. Too many men had drawn water from that well.'

There spoke the colossal egotism of the male sex of those days. Any sexual adventures or diversions were all right for them, but beyond the pale for a woman.

There was Molly Morgan, a woman earning her own living

in a responsible job, but always referred to by William and Albert as 'Molly Morgan', never Miss or Mrs; while the head porter—equally licentious if not more so—was always 'Mr Palmer', never 'that dirty old man, Arthur'.

'Almost every night, when I had finished work, I used to go straight to William's place, and have a bath. What luxury that was in comparison with washing in the sink at home. William was such a snappy dresser, and he never minded me borrowing his things. Sometimes, when we went out, everything I was wearing belonged to him; I was dressed-up like a ham-bone. I remember once, when we were on the top of an open-deck bus, my hat blew off, and I shouted out, "William, there goes your hat." People gazed at me in amazement. I really used to feel a somebody, I looked so smart. You'd never have recognised me then, Margaret.'

No, nor would I have wanted to. I have never forgotten the apparition that greeted me the first time I saw Albert out of his milkman's gear. He was wearing fawn spats, yellow chamois gloves, a fly-away bow tie and carrying a silver mounted walking stick. Talk about a poor man's Beau Brummel, William's idea of the smart man definitely wasn't mine.

William's two sisters were both cooks in domestic service, and liked being there. Eventually, Mary was left five pounds a week for life, and Lottie was left a lump sum of £2,000, when her employer died. They too, like William, never married, although Mary was quite good-looking.

'Many were the hectic evenings that William and I spent in the servants' hall either at Mary's place or Lottie's. We'd all sit round the table after supper discussing the vagaries of "them upstairs". Or the butler and valet would swop stories about the different masters they had worked for. These stories would get more and more vulgar. Our supper parties generally ended by Mr Moore, the butler, offering 2/6d for the smuttiest story. None of the female servants seemed to mind listening. As for me,' Albert went on, 'for every ribaldry that Mr Moore uttered, I could nearly always cap it, so I got many a half-crown. That Mr Moore was a card. I often wondered why William's sister Mary didn't marry him.'

Ladies didn't mind their butler marrying the cook—it often meant that they got two servants more cheaply—but they were not keen on his marrying any one other than a servant, and wanting to live out. Obviously it would mean that his mind wasn't solely on their affairs.

Butlers were really the élite of 'below stairs'. Even the cook called the butler 'Mr' and not by his first name. By spending so much of their time 'above stairs' butlers acquired a slow and dignified way of speaking to those under them. Both the butler and the cook were made much of by the tradesmen. The cook because it was she who chose the butcher, fishmonger, dairy, etc., and the butler because it was he who often advised his employer on choosing and buying the wine.

When I was a kitchenmaid I was always in awe of butlers, but not so my friend Gladys, the under-housemaid. In the privacy of our shared bedroom she would take off the pompous manner of our butler, Mr Rogers, until we collapsed with laughter. Mr Rogers was always talking about the superiority of Englishmen. 'We are the bulldog breed,' he would proudly declare. On one of these occasions Gladys whispered to me, 'I reckon his Dad mated with a French poodle.' I nearly choked with trying not to laugh. Gladys was a year older than me, and one of nineteen children. She really was a friend to me. Her father was a docker, and in those days a docker was never certain of a day's work.

I once went to tea at Gladys's home in Stepney; what a revelation it was. There were about ten kids of school age as well as older ones who worked—when there was any work. How they all crammed into those four rooms was a mystery, but everybody seemed happy. Her Mother, whose whole married life had been bursting with fecundity, appeared to me to be in imminent danger of producing another off-spring at the table. But Gladys said it was a false alarm. Her Mother's shape was permanently that way after having so many kids. The whole time we were there the younger kids were running in and out with chunks of bread-and-marge in their hands, or bawling that so-and-so next-door had hit them. They got another clump from Mrs Palmer and were told to fight their own battles. Just what my Mother said to us when we quarrelled with neighbouring children. Living so closely packed with the neighbours, as the working-class did it just didn't do to take umbrage if your kid got knocked about by their kids. Otherwise, furious parents would come banging on your door telling you to keep your bloody hands off their Johnny or Mary.

Along our street on Saturday night, fights among the women were a common occurrence. A way of getting rid of the frustrations caused by lack of money, poor housing, too many kids and a husband who got drunk on a Saturday night and wanted to get rid of *his* frustrations by making more kids.

It wasn't only through having children that Gladys's Mother had the appearance of being permanently pregnant. Part of the cause was that, three days after each birth, she was up and about, cooking, washing and scrubbing for the family. She had never once been in a hospital for a baby; had never experienced either ante- or post-natal care—and most certainly wouldn't have had it if it had been offered. Although my Mother gave birth to all seven of us at home, she always had a qualified midwife. Mother also insisted on staying in bed for the allotted ten days of confinement. She was extremely proud of her slim figure and meant to keep it that way. Most of Gladys's brothers and sisters were delivered by an old woman along the street, whose standard of hygiene must have been practically non-existent. When I expressed surprise that none of her babies had died at birth, and that she had never had the doctor in, Mrs Palmer laughed, 'Never needed none of them quacks, my dear. Old Sal knows more about delivering babies than some bloody young man or po-faced nurse who's never had the chance to make one. Old Sal's had a dozen of her own. You have one of those council women round, and before you know where you are they're poking and prying all over your home. Telling you that too many sleep in one room, that you mustn't have a lodger, and what are you doing about the bugs? They even have the bloody nerve to wonder where some of your things come from.'

I too was rather curious, as several items such as an expensive clock, camera and ornaments looked distinctly odd in such poverty-stricken surroundings. I wondered if her kids had 'found them before they were lost'.

'They ain't knock-offs. Presents from my older children. They're a good lot, always buying me something,' said Mrs Palmer complacently. Looking around at this swarm of kids living in these four horribly smelly rooms, should have been enough to put one off marriage for life. Yet somehow, in an obscure way, I couldn't help feeling that the family was worth-while. In spite of occasional cuffs all the children were happy and loved.

'One of the pleasant changes that William made in my life,' said Albert, 'was to show me that there were more ways of spend-ing one's leisure than frequenting pubs and cinemas. On fine weekends we'd cycle into the country; in those days, the country wasn't too many miles outside London. I remember one day, cycling back through New Cross, William's bicycle caught in the tram-line, and threw him clean over the top. He wasn't as badly damaged as the bicycle—which he had borrowed from the store-room, unbeknown to the tenant who owned it. William wrote a highly indignant letter to the borough council on the dangers of tram-lines that weren't level with the road—and he enclosed the bill for repairs. Much to my, and his, astonish-ment, they sent him the money for this bill.

'In the winter evenings we often went to the music halls; the old Chelsea Palace, Shepherds Bush Empire, Holborn and the "Met" in Edgware Road. Incidentally, in the "Met", whenever one needed the loo, and I frequently did as I drank beer in pints, there was an old man there stationed by the loo door. He got no money for this, as it was a voluntary job, though not a labour of love. He made a bit by opening the door for the men, and then holding out his hand for a tip when they came out. Some of them put just a button in his hand. I expect he was an old-age pensioner. But what a job! Commissionaire to an insanitary men's loo in an old music hall. The smell alone was enough to knock one out.

'Naturally, as I was with William, we sat in the stalls; not nearly so lively as the gallery where I used to sit when I went on my own. Up there we'd drink pints of beer in the interval and boo and hiss any turn we considered a flop.'

Chapter 4

It was just after Albert had spent a week's holiday with William in Cornwall that he asked me out for an evening. Albert had long ago left the butcher's and was now working for the Express Dairy. Although I saw him every day when he called on his second round, I had never bothered to have designs on him because I thought he was married. Partly because he is five years older than me—which seems a lot when you are young—but mainly because he very often wore a plain gold ring. In those days, not many married men wore plain gold rings, never mind those who weren't.

I must admit that Albert was very good-looking, tall and slim with masses of dark wavy hair. Perched up on his high milk-float driving a very spirited horse, he reminded me of Ben Hur. I should have remembered that he wouldn't always look like Ben Hur—though he still has a good head of hair. Unfortunately, this asset has never seemed to do as much for Albert, and indirectly for me, as did Samson's locks before he succumbed to the wiles of Delilah.

'Didn't it seem strange to you, going out with a girl again, after all those years with your friend William?' I enquired.

'Not at all. Don't forget that I saw plenty of females while doing my milk-round, and the under-servants where William's sisters worked were always making a fuss of me. They knew I wasn't married.'

At this time I was a temporary cook for a Lady Downall. She was such a charming and kind person, I wished that the job was permanent. We could always borrow books from her library—though none of the servants except me wanted to do so. Totally unlike the author of a book I had read, entitled *Nooks and Corners*, published in 1899. She wrote, 'No servant, no matter

43

who, should ever be allowed to read the library books.'

But Lady Downall belonged to the real aristocracy, and the gap between these and the more prosperous middle-class was as wide, if not wider, than the gap between the middle-class and the poor. My Mother, who worked mostly for the aristocracy, considered they were better employers than the new rich. They were not continually trying to impress you with their superiority, they just knew they were superior.

In houses where there was a huge staff of servants, like those where I was a kitchenmaid, the hierarchy below stairs seemed as rigid as that between the servants and 'them' above. And it caused even more misery to us underlings. The pecking order started with the housekeeper, butler, valet and lady's-maid, so by the time it reached the lowest, the pecks were pretty vicious. I suppose that as 'them' above stairs made the top servants feel inferior, they had their turn of feeling superior by lording it over us. Though I must admit that Mr Wade, the butler in my first place, was very nice and kind to me. He often helped me to carry the heavy scuttles of coal. I didn't know that it was an absolutely unheard-of thing for a butler to do this until the cook, Mrs McIlroy, told me so. He sometimes treated me to the pictures, and once when I accidentally met him out in the evening, he even took me into a pub. I really felt somebody; though slightly deflated when he asked me not to let the servants know. Eventually, he got the sack through drinking too much and too often. Maybe it was the drink that mellowed him and made him feel fatherly towards me.

Gladys, the under-housemaid in the first London job I had, warned me against 'friendly butlers'. 'If they try to do you a favour,' said Gladys, 'say to yourself, "what's in it for them?"; for sure there is something. I've known butlers who seem to imagine they have more seigneurial rights over people like me and you, than the masters do.'

'What on earth are "seigneurial rights"?'

'Oh!' Gladys giggled, 'I've just read about it in this *True Love* magazine. It's all about this young and beautiful village girl with a lovely nature, who was just about to get married to her childhood sweetheart. One day the Lord of the Manor saw

44

and desired her. So, it says here, "he exercised his seigneurial rights". That means he seduced her. He made her go to bed with him. Afterwards, her childhood sweetheart shot the Lord dead. So we have to be careful.'

I just laughed. 'Well, Gladys, we don't need to worry. The only resemblance between that heroine and us, is that we too are young. Our life isn't conducive to a "lovely nature", and we are certainly not beautiful. I don't think we are going to find men queueing up or trampling over each other for a chance to possess one of us.'

I was often surprised by Gladys's romantic nature. Considering her background, Stepney, a docker Father often out of work, and swarms of brothers and sisters, one would have thought romance would be a dead duck to Gladys. Perhaps it was through reading all those love magazines. I soon gave them up; they seemed so rubbishy. But Gladys bought about three every week. She would wax eloquent and sigh over the misfortunes of Clare, Helen or Celia, but as true love nearly always triumphed, Gladys ended up as happy as her heroines. Years afterwards, I heard that she had married the boy next door and was well on the way to emulating her Mother in size of family.

One of the reasons that William was fond of Albert was because Albert, apart from wearing William's clothes, never sponged on him. Nevertheless, going out with William wasn't as expensive as taking a girl out, so over the eleven years of this friendship, Albert had managed to save some money—considerably more than I had. But then, although Albert was very generous to his Mother, as was William, he earned more actual money than I did, as part of my wages was board and lodging. Besides, my Father wasn't earning much of a wage, so I helped out. Anyway, when we got married, Albert was able to pay cash for all our home, except the piano, still a coveted adjunct of a working-class home—even though unplayable by its owners. There wasn't enough money left over to have a white wedding with all the trimmings and dozens of heretofore unknown relations. This suited Albert admirably as he has a rooted objection to entertaining people unless it is a pleasure to meet them. We got married in a registry office, and then went to our Chelsea rooms for a wedding lunch, with just our parents and a few friends—and William of course. That day was one of the rare occasions on which my Father put his arms around me, and kissed me. I was so overcome with emotion that for that moment I loved him more than I did Albert. My Mother was thankful to see me married. She had begun to worry, as had I, that I would remain on the shelf for the rest of my life. In fact, I was so relieved to get my marriage lines that I nearly framed them.

Strangely, my Mother and Albert's Mother, in spite of their different temperaments, got on very well together. My Mother as a direct result of her unknown ancestry, was assertive, determined, and a force to be reckoned with. Albert's Mother, in spite of the hardships of her life with an unsatisfactory husband, was quiet, self-effacing and one of the most uncomplaining people I have ever met. Even later on in life, crippled with arthritis, and with far more than her share of sorrows, she never became bitter about her lot. To lose Albert to me could not have brought her any joy; he had been more than a son to her.

And, with a mother's intuition, doubtless she could sense, especially after talking to *my* Mother, that I wasn't going to be a meek and mild wife, or wait on Albert hand and foot.

We couldn't afford the conventional honeymoon languorously lolling around under the moon, so we had a marvellous week exploring London, and a day at Southend, where, as the tide was out, we gazed at the sea across a seemingly interminable desert of mud. We ate mussels, and had a hilarious time in the fun-fair where I won a pair of ornaments that one hopes only to see in a nightmare. Albert said they were 'colourful'; he couldn't have said a truer word. I so much enjoyed our week. I said to Albert, 'Do you think that people can tell we have just got married?'

I wasn't delighted when he replied, 'Well! They wouldn't if you didn't drape yourself around me all the time. You don't have to keep giving me practical demonstrations of your affection. I know you care about me without that. People, however much in love, don't have to continually assure each other of their affections in a physical way.'

I suppose Albert was right. Certainly my parents, though

46

much in love, gave no visible signs of it. My Mother detested outward shows of private emotions. But I am not so sure. I feel that something is lost when one cannot show love in a physical way. There is a danger of stultifying one's natural impulses, till at the end one is incapable of any form of outward expression of love. Communion of minds is not enough while one is young enough for other forms of contact.

I indignantly berated Albert, saying, 'It's all very well to be Darby and Joan by the fireside when we get older and *our* fires have gone out. But who wants to emulate them in the early days of marriage. Not me, that's for sure.'

The actual mechanics of getting married were easy. It was the adjustment to a different life that posed problems for me. It seemed to me that the only change for Albert was the home venue. He still did the same job, and saw the same people, including his Mother. At that time, I didn't understand, or appreciate, Albert's attachment to his Mother, or how much she had depended on him, for I had been away from *my* home for a long time. Although Albert was the kindest and most easy-going of husbands, it says much for his character and affection for his Mother that, in spite of my caustic comments, he still continued to see her at least three days every week. And his friend William was continually calling round with some addition to our home for which I should have been grateful, but wasn't. I complained to Albert that I didn't inflict my parents or friends on him, and was not consoled when Albert, reasonably enough, said it was only because they were fifty miles distant.

The drawback to our Chelsea home was that, as we had only a tiny kitchen, and one other room in which we also slept, we had to wait until our visitors left before we could change our settee into a bed. If all the maledictions I directed against that William had come to pass, the poor man would have been worse off than Job. Yet I had sense enough not to present Albert with any dramatic ultimatum such as, 'it's either him or me'.

I certainly ought to have been nicer to William. After all, I had gained what he had lost. But daily I would complain to poor Albert: 'Why on earth does he haunt us by coming round

47

here nearly every evening? We don't need his company, we haven't been married five minutes. Marriage is supposed to be a twosome, not a trio. He's had you for eleven years, why doesn't he call it a day?' On and on I went like a needle in the groove of a worn-out record. Yet William was one of the kindest of men, and a very good friend indeed to both of us. Because I couldn't sleep well on the hard mattress of our bed-settee, he bought us a real hair mattress. In the winter he paid for half a ton of coal. I once said how much I liked bone china. Along came a lovely tea-set in such fine porcelain that one could see through it. Nothing was too much trouble for him; I'm very glad that eventually I did make him feel welcome.

We had been married only a few weeks when Albert was taken off his milk-round and, much to his annoyance, given a round that included Maida Vale, where so many 'ladies of the night' lived. The reason the Express Dairy moved Albert was that he was good at reducing bad debts, of which there were many in that district. As well as milk, cream and eggs, Albert had groceries and cakes to sell, so a customer could very quickly run up a large bill. As the ladies' incomes were uncertain to say the least, it was Albert's job to try to get some money—which he did by a mixture of sweet reason and cajolery. In spite of the fact that, married to me, I couldn't see why he should have any inclination to stray, nevertheless I was slightly uneasy when Albert told me that, about 6 o'clock in the morning, he had to call into room after room, to collect the milk money.

'There are these ladies,' related Albert—too calmly I thought —'lying there in bed, topless. Most of them are a very unlovely sight. Hair like a bird's nest, eye-black running and make-up smudged. The rooms reeking to heaven of smoke, cheap perfume and disinfectant. If their night has been a "labour of love", then I find the milk money on the side-board, occasionally even a bit off the back debt.'

I would sometimes wonder whether, when these ladies couldn't pay their bill, they might offer to 'work it off in trade'. Especially as Albert was very nice-looking.

'Don't worry, my love,' Albert reassured me, 'I wouldn't touch them with a barge pole.'

Perhaps not; but it wasn't a barge pole I was worried about.

One morning Albert came home bursting to relate how he had become a Sir Galahad, a Don Quixote and a knight-errant all rolled into one.

'I went into the room of this woman called Mona to collect the milk money and found her having a furious row with a somewhat corpulent and elderly man. He was complaining bitterly that Mona had cheated him, he hadn't had his money's worth. He wasn't leaving until she had returned some of his fee. He was a bit taken aback when I walked in and Mona appealed to me to get him out of her room. "He's been here a bloody hour already," she told me, "what does he think I am, a bloody universal provider. For what he's had he should think himself lucky." '

By this time I was all agog to hear more of this erotic and alien way of life. 'Go on then, what did you do?'

'Well, it was difficult for me to arbitrate as I didn't know what constituted his "money's worth", whether he'd got value or not' —I should hope Albert wouldn't know. 'Anyway, I managed to calm him down and see him off the premises; much to my and Mona's relief. In fact, she was so overcome by my good deed that she actually paid half of the back milk bill.'

'Well, love,' I warned Albert, 'don't get too chivalrous. The next obstreperous customer that she gets may not be corpulent and elderly. I don't want a dead hero, and you wouldn't exactly have died in a good cause. Besides, how come you know this Mona so well?'

'Oh, everybody knows Mona.'

Albert was right too, as I found out when one evening she came into our local pub. Many of the regulars greeted her as an old friend. When she saw Albert she came over without the slightest sign of embarrassment, I was the one who had a red face. Strangely enough, I found that I liked Mona. She was about thirty-five or so, with really lovely green eyes, reddish hair and fair skin not plastered with make-up. Her conversation was, to say the least, somewhat disconcerting.

'Hello, your husband has no doubt told you who I am. I'm a prostitute. It's a job like any other. And if you have read any rubbish about a prostitute having a "heart of gold", forget it. Most of them have a heart like a cash register.'

Mona and I became quite friendly. I think that she liked me as much as one woman can like another. Occasionally, while Albert was on his milk-round, Mona looked in at our place for a coffee and a chat. She was perfectly frank about her life. No rubbish about being seduced and driven to a life of sin. She had willingly walked along that road. Mona found in me an avid listener, always ready for the next episode.

'I was a real country girl,' said Mona. 'My parents were strict chapel-going Bible-thumpers, models of piety and rectitude. They not only believed in the doctrine of "original sin", they also stuffed it down us children from morning to night. How they ever produced a family of five I'll never know. They must have done it by remote control. Our only diversions were Bible reading and prayers; hell-fire awaited us if we so much as wore a bright ribbon in our hair. As for letting us go to the village hops, my Mother would as soon have locked all of us away for life. Our cottage had no running water, gas or light. I tell you, Margaret, my parents couldn't understand how they got *me* with green eyes and red hair. Though once in an old album I saw an ancient photo of a woman with my features and when I asked my Mother who she was, Mother snatched the book away, saying "she was evil".'

'How did you get started on this life, did you run away from home for the city?'

Here Mona giggled reminiscently. 'I'll never forget how I got launched on this "sea of iniquity". I was about fifteen, and, in spite of my Mother's efforts to eradicate or disguise my charms, I was attractive, as I already knew. One evening I was sitting in our parlour alone, the others in bed and my parents in chapel, when a Mr Dent, one of the local farmers, called round to see my Father. He was a huge, beefy, red-faced man with hands like legs-o'-mutton. His favourite expression was, "I'm a plain man and I speak my mind." He sat down on the sofa next to me and just then the oil-lamp went out. Unlike the wise virgins —although I was one then—I had no oil handy. Without warning, while I was trying to find the oil-can in the dark, two enormous hands came round my waist and lifted me off the ground. I was too astonished to make a noise. Then one of the hands started roaming and believe me, Margaret, I really liked the sensation. Still in the dark he sat me on his lap and began a voyage of discovery—I did too. It was very exciting and electrifying. I could have gone on for a long time. Not a word had been spoken since the light went out. Suddenly, up jumped Mr Dent, dumped me on the sofa, put a piece of paper in my hand, and left. I got the oil, lit the lamp and found he had given me five pounds. I nearly fainted. Five pounds! I'd never owned five shillings, up to then. All that money for doing nothing and having pleasure. I hid the money and said not a word to anyone. It was money for old rope.'

As by this time Mona and I were drinking our third glass of the gin she had thoughtfully brought with her, we laughed uproariously. The next time she arrived she continued with the saga of her fall from grace, into original sin—well, perhaps it was ordinary sin.

'The following Sunday, when I saw Mr Dent in chapel, I gave him a malicious side-long glance. He went as red as a turkey-cock, I had hard work to suppress my mirth. To add to his discomfiture he had to read the lesson that Sunday. It was about the evils of fornication and the fiery lake that awaited those who indulged in this vile sin. Nothing could have been more fiery than his face with me gazing soulfully at him as though he was a father-confessor. I believe my Mother thought I had received the call to renounce all worldly aspirations.'

'And had you, Mona?' I enquired, as I encouraged her to continue while drinking a cup of Irish coffee. Not that Mona needed encouragement. She had seldom had such a good listener. As good as lying on the psychiatrist's couch—and considerably cheaper.

'Not on your life. Here I was, a shop assistant earning thirty shillings a week for working all the hours there were, and getting bored to tears in the process; seeing that I could get £5 in a much easier and more enjoyable way was enough for me. Jack Dent came round again; I knew he would once he understood that I wasn't going to split on him. When I had collected enough money I decamped for London. I've never been back or seen my parents since. But I bet my Mother spent even more time on her knees praying for my salvation. If she had spent more time in loving me in this life, and less in being so bloody concerned with my soul, I might still be living an innocent life. Though to be honest, I doubt it.'

Albert wasn't too keen on this friendship with Mona; maybe he was afraid that some of her philosophy would rub off on me. But as he was the original cause of my knowing her, he couldn't say too much. For my part, I was still apprehensive that one of the 'ladies' might lead Albert astray. After all, their sexual prowess must have been greater than mine. It would need to be as they were getting paid for it.

The last time that we saw Mona in our local she looked extremely attractive and prosperous, and as full of life as ever. She told us that she now had a flat of her own, paid for by her latest. 'He's fat, forty and about fifty Fahrenheit in bed, but he's sweet. And best of all I only get him weekends.' In spite of her way of life there was something very likeable about Mona. But when she said, 'Why don't you both come up and see me sometime,' I thought it politic not to. I wouldn't have wanted Albert to go without me; he wasn't *her* milkman.

About this time the branch where Albert worked was reorganised, and some of the men became redundant—including Albert. He was promised a round as soon as there was a vacancy, but it was actually six months' waiting before he got back with the firm; he was just about to go on the dreaded Means Test.

We would have found it difficult to live during this time without William's help. He showered goods on us in abundance. As it was, our only hire-purchase, the piano, had to be given up. I didn't mind too much although I suffered mortification at all the neighbours viewing its exit. In a way the piano was a perpetual reproach and a thorn in the flesh to me. I disliked the proximity of something that made me feel inadequate as I was unable to play it. Poor Albert was very long-suffering indeed when he had to listen to me picking out tunes with one finger. For, unlike me, Albert really does love music—except those profound and gloomy Wagnerian operas.

Chapter 5

It was a very hard time for Albert. He hated being out of work. It was not so much the lack of money, as the feeling of being inadequate, unwanted and ignored. Not by me; I wanted him, I hadn't married him for his money, so to receive an even smaller amount of this necessity caused me no undue grief. I tried to encourage him, saying it wasn't his fault that there was no work about, he'd get a job eventually. I suggested that as he didn't have to get up early for work, we could spend more time in bed, thus using up the time, and providing an enjoyable occupation at minimal cost.

Albert had a mind above such frivolous pursuits. He cycled all over London after real and mythical jobs, sometimes being away all day and arriving back so tired and dispirited, he could hardly speak. I knew how he felt. I had seen it happen so often with my Father. There is nothing more soul-destroying than to find that nowhere is there a place for you; that your loyalty and capacity for hard work are not needed by anybody. Occasionally, Albert did manage to get taken on, but somehow something always seemed to go wrong, so that after a week or two his employers decided they could manage as well without him. He came home once full of excitement because he had got a job in a laundry at £5 per week.

'What sort of job, Albert? What are you doing?'

'Oh, no particular job,' said Albert vaguely, 'just make myself generally useful, a sort of dog's-body.'

What that turned out to mean was that he was at everybody's beck and call. In trying to please all he succeeded only in pleasing none. But he really was told to go after two weeks because he couldn't seem to pull the right switch, although there were only three. The second time he made a mistake, hot water gushed all over the washer-women—their language was even hotter. Albert barely escaped with his life, pursued by four ferocious females. Fortunately he was owed only two days' wages.

'Don't go back, my love,' I sympathised, 'let them keep the two days' money. We can manage.'

I needn't have bothered about being so magnanimous as Albert had no intention of returning to the scene of his humiliation.

He could have had a job exercising two yapping Pekingese dogs. They belonged to a Mrs Swallow, a very wealthy lady who lived in the block of flats where William was a porter. In fact, it was William, completely lacking in savoir-faire, who had recommended Albert to this dog-lover. Albert, without saying anything to me, went round to see her.

'There she sat,' Albert retailed to me at great length later on, 'enclosed in folds of flesh, dressed in a purple robe, reddish hair obviously fake, three double-chins, and podgy hands loaded with diamond rings. She was surrounded by every comfort and luxury that money could buy. Thick carpets, lovely furniture and paint-ings, cut-glass and priceless china. To me she was living the life of Riley. But she complained all the time about the hardships of her life. Service in shops was deplorable, her friends never came to see her, and how she missed her wonderful husband who died ten years ago. "We never had an angry word, he worshipped the ground I walked on. He never in all our married life looked at another woman. He always said there was no one like me." I wondered in what way her husband had meant that.'

'Well, go on,' I said impatiently, 'when are you getting round to those pampered Pekingese?'

'Hold your horses, Margaret, I'm preparing the ground. She then asked me if I liked dogs, opened a door and in came two Pekingese who rushed furiously and intrepidly at me barking loud enough to be heard in Peking. "Ah!" said Mrs Swallow, "they have taken a liking to you."

'You could have fooled me, Margaret. I wondered how they acted to somebody they didn't like. Probably made a meal of them. Anyway, Mrs Swallow said that she could see that I was a nice kind dependable man who would really look after her treasures in the street. Her treasures' names were Wang and

Wung and they were pedigree Pekingese. So what do you think, my love; shall I take the job? It's only an hour morning and evening, and it would help out with the dole.'

I rose up in righteous wrath.

'Albert, perish the day when you have to be associated with two footling little dogs on the end of a lead, loitering and waiting in the streets while those pampered pets make up their minds just which tree or lamp post they will foul. I flatly refuse to have a husband who indulges in such puerile pursuits. In fact, I wouldn't even acknowledge you if I saw you out with them.'

'All right then,' and Albert was really aggrieved. 'I was only doing it for you. You don't imagine that I fancied myself as a dog-toter.'

'Well, Albert, don't bother to do me any more favours like that. And tell that William to keep any more such brilliant ideas for your employment strictly to himself. I know he's a Good Samaritan and all that, but we see enough of him now without you calling at the flats twice a day.'

When Albert turned the job down, that tactless William even had the nerve to suggest to him 'what about Margaret doing the job?' If not for the fact that he was Albert's friend—and at the moment our universal provider—I would have annihilated him. I know that Pekingese are lion-dogs but there is a limit; it wouldn't have been like walking out with two Alsatians or St Bernards. Albert could really have looked a man doing that. Besides, it would never have done; Albert too might have become Mrs Swallow's pet.

Albert was out of work for so long that he began to get anxious and worried at the approaching imminence of the Means Test. So when eventually he got back with the Express Dairy, we felt greatly relieved and thankful. I immediately went out and pawned the only pawnable object I had left, which was a gold locket originally belonging to my grandmother. We went over to our local, the Queen's Elm, and had a small celebration. Unbeknown to me at the time naturally, that small celebration produced a lasting result. I didn't mind, as I wanted to have children, hostages to fortune so to say. Albert wasn't wildly enthusiastic. His own childhood hadn't been one to encourage the desire for family life. But when, after much travail, the baby arrived, an absolute miniature of Albert, he quickly became a proud father. The whole process of having a baby appalled me. The hours it took to arrive were exhausting; from Friday midnight until Sunday midnight—all our children were born on Sundays. The doctor grumbled all the time about the delay. They didn't give one anything to hurry it up in those days. Anybody would have thought it was my fault that he missed his round of golf on Sunday. Personally, he was such a doddery old man I wouldn't have thought he could even see the ball, let alone hit it. Nevertheless, I still think it more comforting to have one's babies at home instead of in a hospital. I was with my own people and could do as I liked. My baby wasn't one of half-a-dozen all born in the same place.

Albert really enjoyed the healthy open-air life of a milk-roundsman. The feeling that once he had started on his round, he was his own boss, as long as he pleased his customers by always being polite and punctual, and satisfied his employers by getting something off the back debts and being a good salesman. This Albert did well, especially the latter, as part of his wages was commission.

Albert wasn't the 'boss' in his own home, but then he didn't want to be. Nobody was the 'boss'. We were partners in the business of making a marriage work. I didn't mind at all the lack of money, the cramped accommodation, the sparseness of our home—I never was keen on material things. Albert was doing the job that he liked, a far more important consideration than the wages. What I wanted above everything was freedom. Freedom to be equal with men, freedom to become somebody in my own right. Never could I visualise myself having to ask my husband if I could go out without him, or if I could indulge in some pursuit in which he had no interest. The time to draw up a set of rules for what you want from your own married life is before the marriage. At that time, presumably, your future husband desires you enough to raise no objections to your proposals. It's no use being married about ten years and then suddenly saying, 'I want to go out twice a week to evening classes.' Of course then your partner will raise the roof; why would he not? In the first place he has got accustomed to seeing you there always. You come in with the furniture—the front room furniture of course. Secondly, it is a reflection on him: that he isn't man enough for you, that he satisfies you neither physically nor intellectually. He becomes, in his opinion, justifiably aggrieved.

'Don't I toil six days a week to keep you in food and clothes? Who keeps the home going? Don't I take you to the pictures every week and the pub on Saturday night? What more do you expect of me?'

When you reply that these delectable diversions are fine, that you are overwhelmed with gratitude for benefits received, that no, certainly you are not fed up with him, that yes, you do appreciate how hard he works for both, but that you feel frustrated at being only a house-wife, you hear the age-old cry, 'why did you marry me then?'

Probably my desire for a life outside the confines of the home was fostered by my Mother. Her love for me increased in direct ratio to the distance between me and my Father. Mother wrote to me about everything. The family, the neighbours, the rapacity of the landlord, and above all, politics. I too was interested in this subject, but could never get Albert to discuss with me the iniquities or advantages of the men in Parliament.

'Why bother your head about all that stuff?' Albert would say. 'It doesn't make any difference who's in, or out. As soon as they are elected they become Jacks-in-office, determined to enjoy their brief moment of power, and the people can go to the devil. I couldn't care less who gets in; they don't provide my bread and butter.'

My Mother wrote to tell me that next time I came down she had a lovely present for me. A well-bound set of Dickens' books —she knew I liked Dickens. All they had cost her was about twelve shillings and coupons from the *Daily Herald*. I too had noticed this remarkable offer, but complete works of any classic, even given free, would not have induced me to read the *Daily Herald*. All the newspapers seemed to be going stark crazy about offering free gifts to increase their circulation, regardless of the fact that when the new reader had acquired enough coupons, he, or she, very soon returned to buying the newspaper they had always read.

Mother wrote that my Father was becoming increasingly disillusioned with the Labour Party. Dad was an ardent Socialist, though never a street-corner ranter or a speaker in working-men's clubs. But my Father had always firmly believed that when a working-class man had a decent job for a decent wage, and a decent home to live in, life would become a kind of Utopia. Dad could never see that the rich hadn't a prerogative of human failings. The poor too could climb over their fellow-men in the desire to rise in the world. The poor too could be hard, ruthless and avaricious, and never be satisfied with their decent home and job. Once, when I went home for a day, I had a long talk with my Father. 'You know, Nell'—they call me Nell at home—'I just cannot believe that Ramsay MacDonald could be such a traitor as to leave the Labour Party. He was the working-man's saviour, a Daniel come to judgment. How could he betray us now? What has changed him? We all trusted him, believed in the words that poured out in support of the poor and downtrodden, the ill-paid toilers. That Ramsay MacDonald should join hands with Baldwin, with Chamberlain and Sir Herbert Samuel, has made me so disillusioned, Nell, that I have finished with the lot of them. They are all corrupt; even those who were like us, ill-educated and humiliated.'

Poor Dad, he was far too much of an idealist and a dreamer to live comfortably in an ever-increasingly materialistic world.

My Mother, who always had strong feelings about anything that concerned my Father, was torn between sorrow that Dad's illusions were shattered, and impatience that he ever had them in the first place. Mother's firm opinion was that 'only the poor help the poor', and all the pre-election promises of aspiring candidates ended up as 'castles in the air, and palaces built of shifting sand'. Mother often came out with these flowery phrases; she got them out of books, I know. So do I.

When a National Government was formed, my Mother attempted to console my Father, 'You see, Harry, it has to be to save our gold. Just imagine the catastrophe that would follow if we went off the gold standard. I agree with you, Harry, about the perfidiousness of that Ramsay MacDonald, but you don't want to see the country ruined, do you?'

So when, about a month later, the country went off the gold standard, I thought my Mother would have apoplexy with indignation and rage. She wrote to me at this time, 'Four years of war, money pouring out in millions for men and armaments, never any shortage of the pound, never a whisper of bankruptcy in war, when money is spent that produces no returns. Now Snowden cannot balance his budget. It's not enough, all the sacrifices we made in the war, now we have to take more. I tell you, Nell, the country is ruined.'

The fact that the country didn't collapse when we abandoned the gold standard in no way appeased my Mother's wrath; if anything it exacerbated it—as did all events that proved her wrong.

Albert was completely unmoved by any of these world-shaking affairs. He had enough of his time taken up in listening to the trials and tribulations of his customers. Of an evening he would sit down and tell me at great length and in detail of his customers and their problems. As I knew none of them, and could not feel particularly concerned, I sometimes used to get really irritated, feeling that if he listened to me as much as he did to his customers, I might become a good conversationalist. One evening, Albert said to me,

'You remember me telling you about a Mrs Blair?'

I didn't remember at all, as most of what Albert said, unless it concerned me, never registered.

'You must remember,' Albert replied impatiently, 'Alice Blair, I've often mentioned her. She has a miserable life with that husband of hers. Would you invite her round to tea? She's so poor and down-trodden. You would cheer her up.'

'For heaven's sake, Albert. You *have* left school, you know. You are not bringing back homework now. Besides, we too are poor. You can't say that we are living in the lap of luxury on your four pounds per week, even with a pint of milk thrown in.'

Though I must confess that Albert was very generous, giving me nearly all his wages every week, and paying for our one evening out with the tips he got.

'I know you are poor, my love, but nobody could say you are down-trodden.'

'Yes, but why me, Albert? Alice Blair would probably far rather have you to console her.'

'It's not a bit like that. She's much older than us, must be nearly fifty. She's got no friends at all. I wish you would talk to her.'

Although I didn't see myself as a sympathetic adviser, I agreed to invite poor, forlorn Alice to tea. When I saw her, I could very well understand just why she was so forlorn and down-trodden. Her whole appearance, proclaiming as it did her meek and martyred nature, was an open invitation to an aggressive husband to down-tread her. Dowdily dressed, mousey hair scraped into a hard bun, she was the complete negation of femininity. I just couldn't imagine what she and I could discuss. What could we have in common except that we were married? Over the tea-cups Alice spoke about Albert. How nice and cheerful he was, even in the foulest of weather. Always so obliging; why, only yesterday he had put a washer on her tap, and another day he had mended a fuse. How lucky I was to have such a good husband. If only her Stan was half as good as my Albert. Getting somewhat bored with this eulogy about a person I saw every day, I said, 'Well, I *am* lucky to have Albert. But he is also lucky to have me. In fact, I consider that most men are lucky who manage to acquire a wife. Certainly it costs them a bit more than it would to live with their Mother. But for the extra pay-out, they get a cook, housemaid, valet and errand boy all rolled into one. All their material wants are satisfied, and, all being well, most of their physical ones. Though I flatly refuse to agree that it always has to be when "they" want to.' I could tell that such heretical opinions were shocking Mrs Blair.

'Is that why, Mrs Powell, you don't wear a wedding ring?'

'I don't wear a wedding ring, partly because I'm allergic to rings of any kind, and partly because men don't have to wear one, and I have a strong aversion to wearing a badge that proclaims to all and sundry that I belong to somebody. I don't belong to anybody. I'm me, and Albert's another person. We have our own rights. Furthermore, Albert doesn't in the least mind that I don't wear a ring.'

Mrs Blair sighed deeply. 'Oh, Mrs Powell, I do wish my Stan

was like your Albert. It must be so lovely to have a husband that cares about you. Makes life worthwhile; it must do.'

By this time I was feeling so exasperated by the ineptitude of this woman, that I determined her Stan was going to see a change in his Alice. I would transform her.

'Mrs Blair—I'm going to call you Alice if you don't mind—why don't you come to my afternoon class once a week? It would do you good. Take your mind off your troubles. There are about twenty-five of us there, all quite lively. It's only for two hours, from 2.30 till 4.30. On the way back some of us call in at Joe Lyons for a cup of tea.'

'Oh, Mrs Powell. It sounds lovely. But I couldn't. Stan would be furious. Suppose I was late home and his tea wasn't ready. No, my Stan would never allow me to do it.'

I nearly exploded with indignation.

'What do you mean, wouldn't allow it? What are you, Alice, an object, a contraption that your Stan winds up and sets to go here and there at his command? You've already told me that he doesn't physically assault you. Surely you can ignore his tongue. Anyway, I would see that you weren't late home. Stan would never know you had been out. Go on, be daring for once. And do call me Margaret.'

'Oh! Margaret, it would be lovely.'

Most of Alice's conversation consisted of 'oh! it would be lovely'.

'What is your class, Margaret? What are you doing?'

'We are learning about the Romantic Revival in literature and art,' I said somewhat pompously.

'Oh, Margaret, it sounds lovely! I adore romance! I take *Peg's Paper* every week! The stories are lovely! Last week there was a beautiful, and yet so sad story about this lovely young girl, Rosalind. She was in love and engaged to a lovely young man. But because she knew that her sister was in love with him this Rosalind left home and went right away so that her sister could have the young man, Duncan. And this Duncan found out where Rosalind was and brought her back because he loved her so much, and not the sister really. Oh! it was a lovely story, I cried all the time.'

I almost choked. But not with emotion, with laughter at Alice's idea of what our class on the Romantic Revival was about.

'It's not quite like that, Alice, but you will get to understand. Try it with me,' I said very gently.

My persuasion managing to overcome her timidity, Alice and I went together for several weeks. I don't believe she ever really grasped that the Romantic Revival was a kind of revolt against classicism to a more imaginative style. Nevertheless, she enjoyed the company, she was one of a group instead of being a nobody. Alice really relished the get-together in Joe Lyons. This was her undoing, for, lingering too long one afternoon, her Stan arrived home before she did. Great was his consternation and fury at finding no Alice, no tea on the table, or kettle on the gas. He just couldn't believe it; things like that could never happen to him. Nobody would dare to alter the pattern of his life. I discovered all this when Stan came round to see the person who had lured his mate from her wifely duties. I felt sure he would come and warned Albert. 'It's all your fault, Albert. It comes of your feeling sorry for her. You have stirred up a hornet's nest. You'll have to cope with the irate husband.'

'My love,' Albert replied, 'I shall hide in the loo. I back you to deal with any man, irate or otherwise. Besides, I didn't ask you to take Mrs Blair to your classes. I said invite her to tea and sympathy.'

When I saw that Stan, I was extremely surprised. From the description Alice had given me I had envisaged a somewhat beery, red-faced and raucous-voiced individual. But Stanley was tall and slim, and not at all bad-looking. I invited him into the living room—Albert was nowhere to be seen—and immediately attacked verbally.

'I know why you're here, Mr Blair, and it's all your fault. You go out to the pub every night leaving your wife on her own; you gamble; you never take her out or even notice her existence. Small wonder that at last she decided to do something for herself. You can't surely begrudge her two hours of freedom one afternoon a week. What are you? A husband or a jailer?'

I expected to be almost annihilated after this denunciation, but was astounded to hear Mr Blair laughing; I just couldn't believe it.

'Oh, Mrs Powell, if only my wife was like you, I'd never go outside the door; I'd be too busy'—I wonder what he meant? 'But you've seen my wife. I ask you, could one take any pleasure in showing her to one's friends? I bet she told you her life is one long martyrdom, how poor and down-trodden she is. Well, she invited it. That meekness is enough to send any man up the wall. As for any excitement in bed, I might as well make love to an old sack; in fact sometimes I feel that is just what I am doing. She'd like me to be castrated; it would be one less indignity for her to bear. She doesn't have to dress as though she can only afford jumble: I give her eight pounds a week.'

Eight pounds a week; an incredible sum. Why, Albert's whole wage was only four pounds. Whatever did Alice do with all that money? I began to feel that Mr Blair wasn't nearly as bad as his wife made him out to be. At least he was generous with house-keeping money. I offered him coffee, which he accepted with alacrity, and then he asked where was my husband.

Albert had kept out of sight only because he knew that I pre-ferred to manage on my own, and that I would exercise more charm than he could—or would want to. So, turfing Albert out of the loo, we all had an amicable discussion about life, marriage and what made people tick. By the end of the evening Stan said he didn't mind in the least if Alice came to the class with me. If he had been free, he would have come too.

I could tell that Albert liked Stan, because Stan listened to Albert's anecdotes and laughed in all the appropriate places. I find it difficult to laugh at a story I have already heard at least three times. Albert told him to drop in whenever he was round our way. I was all set to get furious that I hadn't been consulted as to whether I also wanted the company, but then I thought, Stan will be a change from William.

All should have been well but, unfortunately, Stan seemed to think he had carte blanche to call in whenever he was round our way. And it somehow happened that he had to be round our way about nine o'clock in the morning when Albert was on his milk-round. I didn't mind on the first or second occasion; I made coffee and conversation. But after that, enough's enough. I felt apprehensive of his roving eye, I knew the symptoms. Before long it becomes a roving hand. When I told Albert, he only laughed as he said, 'Oh, don't worry about old Stan. He's only fooling you, just joking. He's as safe as houses. I know you are well able to take care of yourself with old Stan.'

How could Albert be so blind and not see any danger? I was torn between fury that Albert should think Stanley wouldn't find me desirable, and gratification that Albert trusted me. However, I decided the best plan would be to transform Alice from a shapeless object to a recognisable form of womanhood. I was sure that I could do it too. On the way home from our class I started my campaign.

'Alice, you'll never guess what that nice couple in the back row were saying about you. They were asking me where we both lived and then they went on to say to me, "You know, your friend wouldn't be bad-looking if she dressed up a bit. She has such a clear complexion."' Alice did have too; I had noticed that. She visibly brightened when I remarked on this. 'Oh! do you really think so? Did they really say that about me? Well, aren't they nice.'

The couple in the back row hadn't actually spoken about Alice in just that way. What they had really said was, 'For heaven's sake, why on earth does that friend of yours wear such appalling clothes? We wouldn't be seen dead in such a conglomeration of garments; and she's not that bad-looking.'

A few weeks of this praise passed. Then came the day when Alice asked me to go shopping with her for a new dress. I found that she had £250 in Post Office savings. Just imagine, £250, a small fortune.

'Before you buy a dress, Alice, you need a good foundation garment. Something that will give you shape. Then we'll go to the C & A; you could afford two or three dresses from there. And a couple of pairs of shoes, you have such a nice foot, it's a pity to wear those shapeless objects you have on.' Alice did have a dainty foot. She took only size four as against my seven and a half. We bought all these clothes; I gave her a colour shampoo and set her hair, and honestly, I really felt proud of my handiwork. A complete metamorphosis had taken place. No longer 'poor Alice', she definitely felt and looked like a woman. But it was with some trepidation that we waited for Stanley to come in for his tea. I had primed her. 'Now Alice, for goodness sake, don't look like a sick cow when he comes in. Just say, Hello Stan, in a casual way, ask him if he's had a good day and then get the tea. Whatever happens, don't be apologetic. If Stan doesn't like your get up, tell him to take a running jump in the canal or follow your old clothes into the dustbin. With your new look, be a new woman. And remember what I have told you. When he gets ready to go to the pub tonight, you tell him you are going too. Either with, or without him, but the former preferably.'

We needn't have worried. When Stanley had got over the initial shock he was delighted with the alteration. Alice really did look something, and it was 'all my own work too'. Mind you, Stan was no fool. He knew why I had taken all that trouble. He knew that Albert and I didn't want to lose him altogether, as we would have done had he continued his early morning visits to me.

When he called round the next morning to say that he still couldn't believe it was the real Alice, I gave him a warning. 'You do your part now, Stan. Be attentive, praise Alice, don't let her fall back into slipshod ways. And for heaven's sake, when you go to bed, don't rush at it like a bull at a gate; love-making is supposed to be enjoyable, not a physical chore that you need to get over in the shortest possible time. Take a bit of trouble over the preliminaries.'

'Why,' Stan enquired, somewhat maliciously I thought, 'does Albert?'

Hastily informing him that I had no intention of discussing my love life, I changed the subject.

When I found that a second baby was on the way I broke the 'glad tidings' to Albert after he had had a few pints in our local on Saturday night. For I knew that his reception of the news would bear no resemblance to that of the loving husbands in romantic novels. There, the husband, after his dear little blushing wife has whispered in his ear that their union is going to be blessed—why she should blush I don't know, presumably she did her part and knew what was going on—that romantic husband tenderly escorts his wife to the nearest armchair and rushes to get a stool for her feet. Considering that she generally had about another seven months to wait until the results of their blessed union arrived, I used to think that these tokens of solicitude were somewhat premature. Nothing like that occurred with Albert. When I told him that our union was going to receive another blessing—or words to that effect—all I heard was, 'Blimey, not another one already. This place will be like a rabbit warren before long.'

How charming, how nice to feel I was going to be pampered and cosseted—and what a hope. Of course Albert could see that we would no longer be able to stay in our tiny Chelsea flat, nor afford the rent for a larger one in the same district. I must admit that Albert was simply marvellous in the way he searched for somewhere for us to live. Every afternoon after he had finished his second round, he'd bicycle through street after street searching for rooms to let. Eventually he found a place in Willesden, three rooms on the top floor for the same rent as we were paying in Chelsea. There was a family of father, mother and three kids on the middle floor, and a couple of adults on the ground, all those people, together with us three, soon to be four—eleven of us, all sharing one lavatory in the yard, and naturally no bath or hot water. I loathed the place at first. Willesden seemed a dreary environment, no beginning or end to it, and just a dusty park for recreation. What a prospect after the lovely embankment at Chelsea! Of course I got used to it, even began to like it. Certainly I got to like the people and the little family corner shops. Stan and Alice were still our friends as, needless to say, was William.

Just before we moved, Albert's holiday was due. Mother invited us to stay with them for a week. So long as we bought our own food, she would do the cooking. My parents were living in a council house by then. Albert was not overly enthusiastic about the prospect of close contact with my Mother for a whole week, though he could have lived for ever with my Father. In fact I cannot imagine anybody who couldn't live with my Dad. He was so kind and gentle, so unassuming, and yet always ready to talk or give advice if somebody really needed him.

Although I was not an easy person to live with, Albert hardly ever got annoyed with me or raised his voice in anger. But on the rare occasions when he did, one of the worst remarks he could make, was, 'Pack it up Margaret, pipe down. You are getting just like your Mother.'

Albert didn't mean that, like Mother, I was bright, alert and avid for knowledge. He meant the remark in a derogatory sense, that, also like Mother, I was getting aggressive and self-opinionated. However, as regards the holiday, I pointed out to Albert the benefits that would accrue. I would have no cooking to do we would have the pleasures of fresh air, sunshine, sea and sand.

'What sand? Where is it? All I have ever seen on Hove beach is stones, and there's always a howling gale blowing so that you can't even sit on the stones with any comfort. Furthermore, I dislike displaying my torso to all and sundry.'

'Some people are born moaners, Albert. Anyway, I want to go. I care about my parents as much as you do about your Mother.'

My parents were delighted to have us and Harry, who was now about eighteen months and an exceedingly attractive child. He was only their second grandchild so naturally they were enthusiastic. Later on in life, when Mother acquired thirteen grandchildren, and twenty great-grandchildren, the novelty wore off.

My Father by now was working for the council; not a very well-paid job but at least it was regular. And with about two million unemployed, to have regular work was to be extremely lucky. Dad was by now resigned to the fact that his Utopian world would never be, but Mother was still fulminating against Ramsay MacDonald, and against Baldwin too. Both, in her opinion, had been traitors to their party and promises.

'That Ramsay MacDonald,' Mother indignantly rattled on, 'it's nothing else with him but travelling here and there all over the world at the tax-payers' expense, as though he was some Indian potentate. All he does is talk and talk his honeyed words, and when you sift them, he has said nothing. As for Baldwin, mark my words, that man will lead the country to destruction.' Proper Cassandra was my Mum; ready to prophesy at the drop of a hat.

Albert, when we were on our own, said, 'I do wish that you would let your Mother know we are down here on a holiday. If England's going under because nobody asked your Mother to form a Government, it's not my fault. I only wish for all our sakes that she *was* there. I do believe that she would do a lot more good than some of those retired aldermen. But do tell her not to practise on us, Margaret. I'm sure the country will last our week out.'

I was up in arms at once that he should criticise my Mother; especially after she had invited us down. I understood Mum. When you see incompetence and ignorance all around it does tend to irritate.

Our first morning on Hove beach was somewhat of a disaster, albeit at the time an hilarious one. First of all, our Harry screamed blue murder at the sight of all that water; he wouldn't go anywhere near it. I was exceedingly mortified, as another small child on his first visit to the seaside took to it—in the fond words of his doting parents—as though he was one of the original Water Babies.

I had bought Albert a very fetching pair of swimming trunks, dark red with navy blue stripes. He had already informed me that he would much have preferred a costume that covered him up, even perhaps with long sleeves. I took his point when I saw him in those brief trunks; all that exposure of dead-white flesh was somehow obscene. Albert dashed madly over the stones to get under the water, leaving his new brown shoes at the water's edge. Unfortunately, an extra large wave rolled up and swamped the shoes. Albert's usual calm disposition, already irritated by the sea and stones, exploded into fury. It was funny to see him standing there red in the face with rage, in those short swimming trunks, dangling a pair of shoes which were dripping sea-water. I collapsed with laughter; so did the parents of the aforesaid child paragon. The shoes were never the same again. But then neither was Albert as far as the seaside was concerned. The sudden shock of all that cold water had set up a total resistance to repeating the act. However, we became quite friendly with the two who laughed. They were Londoners who lived in Bethnal Green. Mr and Mrs Briggs were convinced that only in London could one really live. The noise, crowds and smoky air were pure oxygen to them.

'We have only come down here for Theodore's health,' Mrs Briggs told me.

Theodore, what a name to give a child in Bethnal Green. The Briggs seemed rather elderly to have such a young child, but later on in the week, when we were having a drink in our local, Mrs Briggs told me that Theodore was a late arrival.

'He was pretty near too late. I got married at twenty, had two daughters by the time I was twenty-five, and fifteen years later had Theodore. I couldn't believe it when the doctor told me I was expecting. I'd thought it was middle-age spread. When I realised it was true I felt the event as much of a miracle as the Virgin Mary must have done. I tell you Mrs Powell, I definitely thought my old man was past it. He is ten years older than me and not exactly love's young dream in bed.'

'Still, I suppose Mr Briggs did contribute to the miracle?'

'Oh sure, but how he managed it is still a bit of a mystery. I put it down to the dandelion wine. Have you ever drunk any?'

I hadn't at the time, but since I have been around talking to Institutes and Guilds I have sampled many home-made wines, and they can be very potent if kept long enough. Occasionally, they can be foul, as was some parsnip wine I was once given; I swear that it had only just left the parsnip.

Mrs Briggs continued, 'We both wanted a son, and just couldn't understand why no more children arrived after the two girls. I was sure that it wasn't me. All my side of the family are terrific producers. I got everything for my Joe; Guinness and port, wine eggs, and butter galore. As for all those pills that are advertised to increase a man's potency, poor old Joe swallowed enough to make him jump around like a buck rabbit. I tell you, the night became our main time of activity; paid work was only incidental. After all, I was only twenty-six.'

'What about the dandelion wine that did the trick?'

'I'm coming to that. Years after we had given up all hope of increasing our family we went on a firm's outing to Epsom.

69

There were two charabancs of us and loads of beer in crates as well as what we consumed over dinner. Suddenly, Joe remembered that he had an old aunt living about a mile away in a little village, whom he hadn't seen since he was a kid. So, being more than slightly sozzled, we decided to visit her. I can't say that she was delighted to see two total strangers, both weaving about somewhat, neither did she manifest any joy when Joe told her he was "Mabel's son". However, she invited us in and gave us a drink of this dandelion wine, which we thought bloody awful, hogswash. Like a couple of bloody hypocrites, we said it was delicious, so his aunt gave us the rest of the bottle to take home, more to get rid of us than out of kindness I suspect. Just before we went to bed, still feeling distinctly merry, we finished up that dandelion wine—dandelions are called piss-a-bed where I was born in Suffolk. My God. It did more than piss-a-bed; it put new life into Joe that night, and into me, as I discovered about three months afterwards. So you stick to dandelion wine, Mrs Powell, if you want a family.'

Trying to get a family wasn't my problem. It was how to prevent having too large a one. Many and weird were the tales I heard of how to have all the pleasures without the pains. Some of the methods must have taken so long to put into effect that I should think all desire and capability would have evaporated. Until the advent of birth-control clinics, the only safe way of making love was rather like having a bath with your socks on— at least that's what Albert said.

Mum was very good to us that week. She worked very hard to make us comfortable, did all the cooking and looked after the child so that Albert and I could go to a film. Even Albert admitted that Mum had qualities he hadn't noticed before. Now that I had a man of my own, Mother didn't get so irritated at Dad's affection for me. I told her about the expected happy event, and having to move from Chelsea. Mum was always very philosophical about events, however catastrophic, that couldn't be averted.

'Well, Nell, whether you want another child or not, it's too late to do anything about it now. So don't bother to take any pills. The time for that was immediately following the night you forgot to take precautions; long before you knew for sure. Anyway, what sort of a family is one child? You need at least two. And things are gradually improving for us working-class. Get rid of some of those in Parliament, Baldwin especially'—Mum didn't know then that he would soon become Premier for a third time.

My Mother used to irritate us and her neighbours by telling them that there would be another war. 'You mark my words; the League of Nations is a total failure, the members couldn't say boo to a goose. Japan is already fighting China and even America is doing nothing about it; Germany is re-arming and getting away with it. All the League does is make hot air and placatory noises.'

In the event, my Mother was right, of course. The fact that her predictions came true didn't endear her to the listeners.

Chapter 6

We returned to London and moved from our Chelsea flat over to Willesden; I was agreeably surprised, and touched, when Mrs Briggs came all the way from Bethnal Green to take Harry off my hands while we got straight. How kind people were in those days; 'love your neighbour' seemed to be the rule rather than the exception. I certainly found our surroundings very different from Chelsea, dull, drab, and depressing, until I began to make friends.

As Albert was still doing the same round, the only hardship that he suffered apart from having to pedal his ancient bicycle further—was having to give up the dart-matches in one of our locals; thank heaven for small mercies, I thought. Albert and William were experts at darts, and innumerable boring Saturday nights I had spent in the pub watching those two enthusiasts. They played as partners, challenged two other dart maniacs, and the losers bought a round of drinks for all four, while the winners took on two more men. The more beer that Albert drunk, the better his throws, so he and William seemed to go on playing all the evening. As no women were allowed to join in this, at that time, essentially male recreation, I'd sit in the bar among a lot of females, fed up to the teeth. Definitely not my idea of a social evening. I like mixed company. Occasionally, when Albert could spare a thought for me and time from knocking back his own pints, he would bring me a drink, a beaming smile and a fatuous remark such as 'You all right, my love?' Of course I wasn't all right, but what could I do? Albert was so obviously enjoying himself. If all the silent execrations that I directed towards Albert had taken effect he'd never have got a double-top, let alone a bull's-eye. To aggravate my already injured feelings, when we got back home, Albert and William, flushed with success—and beer—expected me to cook them bacon and eggs or some other little luxury. As William had usually paid for this I couldn't refuse, though inwardly consigning him to perdition. Once, Albert and William trounced the reigning champions of another pub. So great was their jubilation, you'd have imagined they were playing All England. When, after much celebrating of this momentous occasion, we finally got to bed, Albert said complacently, 'Well love, that showed them a thing or two. They really thought they had the measure of William and me. What an unwelcome surprise they got tonight.'

'Yes, fine, Albert dear,' I replied. 'Now what about giving me a surprise tonight? There's more to life than being an expert at darts. What about using some of that finesse that goes into your delicate throws, on an entirely different game—one that I can join in for a change.'

My frustration and fury were beyond words when I discovered that these honeyed and suggestive remarks of mine had never reached their objective. Albert was already fast asleep. Consigning him, William and darts to Dante's lowest depths of Hell, I got up and consoled myself with a cup of strong tea.

My misfortune was that Albert had never read the books written by Marie Stopes and Havelock Ellis, that I placed in a prominent position by the bed. Nevertheless, as hope springs eternal in the human breast, I still had visions that one night Albert would surprise me; that I would have to switch on the light to see if I had the right man. So far, I had never needed to press that switch.

The family on the floor immediately below us had the unlikely name of Bumbelow. Daisy Bumbelow lived in a perpetual cloud of steam from her everlasting washing. Her three children, of whom the youngest was ten months and the eldest not much over three, were by no means the pride and joy of their parents' life. The baby, Violet—anything less like a violet I have seldom seen—bawled incessantly, especially at night. Daisy said it drove Dick (Mr Bumbelow) nearly mad. The baby's noise didn't do me much good either, though Albert never heard it; that man could sleep through an earthquake. Dick Bumbelow might have been driven to distraction by his children, but not to the extent of avoiding the risk of making more. Daisy was already expecting again. I liked Daisy, she had a simple nature. Far from being a shrewish wife, as others might have been with all those harassing kids and a husband who did nothing to alleviate the hard work at home, Daisy seldom grumbled.

'Well, that's life, Margaret; though I never thought that this would be mine. But as my old Mum was always saying, "You've made your bed, now you've got to lie on it." Though,' and here Daisy would giggle, 'I never realised that Dick would want to lie on it so often.'

Daisy and her kids were the bane of the pre-natal clinic that we both attended once a week, though I very soon stopped going. All that half-undressing in full view of everybody and then waiting around, carrying your underwear in a little bag, to be examined and prodded as though one were a suspect carcass of beef, wasn't my idea of how to have a baby. Daisy never minded, partly because she never had to wait around very long. Her three kids made so much noise that the staff hastened to get rid of her as quickly as possible. We used to push our prams around the dusty park, and a peculiar sight we must have presented. Both of us were so obviously in the family way. Neither Daisy nor I could afford to buy the kind of clothes that would have helped to disguise our condition. Still, we both laughed a lot. One day I said to Daisy, 'I read in the paper this morning that statistics prove that far more men than women have high blood-pressure when making love, and it makes them go bald. Shall we earnestly beseech our husbands to give it all up before it's too late? At the moment they both have a good head of hair.'

Daisy laughed so much I became alarmed that her fourth 'treasure', due before mine, might arrive prematurely. Mr Murphy, the policeman whom we often met in the park and who was a great friend of ours, stopped to enquire about our mirth. When we told him, he took off his helmet and disclosed that his head was almost as bald and shiny as a billiard ball. Naturally that set us off again.

Mr Murphy was such a nice man. His parents still lived in County Cork, where he was born. He explained to us that it wasn't too much sex that had made him bald; he wasn't even married. 'But sure my Father was the finest man in Ireland, and I wanted to be just like him. So you see my dears, one day I kissed the Blarney Stone and made a wish: "Let me be just like me Dad". Sad it was that me dear old Dad was as bald as a coot, so I lost all me hair overnight.'

A great one for blarney was our Mr Murphy.

When I told Daisy that I hadn't had Harry vaccinated and didn't intend to have the new baby done either, she decided that she would do the same, because the vaccination upset the kids for days and made life even more harrowing.

'You have to get a form signed, Daisy, to say you have objections to vaccination. It has to be signed by a magistrate, doctor or Justice of the Peace, and has to be done soon after birth.'

Daisy, scared of anything that included the word 'justice'—having met with so little of it in her life, though I pointed out it was a Justice of the *Peace*—decided on the doctor.

Poor Albert wasn't exactly having a peaceful, harmonious and cheerful life at this time. Not only did he miss his dart sessions, he had me to contend with. My disposition was never angelic while waiting for a new arrival. Partly because I had strange fads and fancies for delicacies impossible to attain. Partly because of the impossibility of looking attractive while wearing the same old clothes. Albert, as far as character went, was an extremely easy man to live with, kind, affectionate and very seldom bad-tempered. But he would never be put upon, not even by me. To add to his discomforts, while he was trying to lay some linoleum in the kitchen the corner of it scraped his eyeball, causing intense pain, and he had to wear an eye pad It was no easy task cycling all that way to work and doing a milk-round with one eye covered. So life wasn't made happier when I complained that Albert hadn't laid the lino properly.

'The pattern doesn't match, Albert, and it isn't even flat. Look at all the little hillocks. In next to no time it will be cracking.'

'How could anybody make a good job of it in this room?' Albert replied, irately. 'None of the walls are true. Anyway,' he added, looking at me, 'it's not the only hillock around here.'

This remark did nothing to lighten the prevailing gloom. I

merely brooded and decided that having a baby was a greatly over-rated pastime. So when Mrs Briggs invited us over for tea one Sunday, we accepted with pleasure. We were surprised to find that, unlike us, they had a whole house in Bethnal Green. Three up and three down, with a bath in the kitchen. Joe (Mr Briggs) had made an ingenious arrangement whereby a board let down over this bath to make a large kitchen table, which we all sat around for tea. I must admit, it was slightly disconcerting not to be able to get one's feet underneath comfortably, but for us it was only a temporary discomfort. Mrs Briggs's old widowed Father lived with them. He was eighty-seven, and a more crusty, crabby and cantankerous old man I had never met. It says much for her, and Joe too, that they endured his caustic tongue and were still kind to him. In his highly improbable youth he had been in the Merchant Navy and, finding in Albert and me a new and captive audience, he proceeded to monopolise the entire conversation with a long, and to my mind, mainly fictitious account of all the places he had seen and the adventures that had befallen him.

'I've seen life, I have. I've been in Australia, I've been in Argentina, I've been in China, I've been in Japan; you name it, I've been in it. I remember once in China, we were sailing down the Yangtse river, when a junk full of pirates tried to ram us. I was on watch at the time and gave the alarm. We very soon put paid to that lot of yellow scum, I can tell you. I myself knocked two of them overboard, although they came at me with cutlasses. I tell you, I've knocked around the world, I have.' He'd also knocked his wife around, literally, and now he'd retired, was knocking his daughter around metaphorically by his unceasing demands on her time. Doris surely was of the stuff of which heroines were made.

Later on, while her Father was crouched over the television set, Doris told me, 'My Mother departed this life, quite cheerfully, four years ago when she was eighty-two. Mother said to me, "I've had fifty years of your Father and now I'm ready for a bit of peace. I'd prefer to dwell up above, but if the good Lord decides to forgive your Father all his sins, and finds a place for him up there, then I'd much sooner go down below." We fully intended to put Dad into a home, but somehow we couldn't bring ourselves to do it.'

When we moved into their sitting room, Albert's eyes brightened at the sight of a dart-board on the wall; and mine at all the shelves of books.

'They all belong to Joe,' Doris proudly told me. 'He went to night school to learn engineering and history. He can read any kind of book, especially biographies. I'm no good at all, I read only romantic novels.'

It was decided we should all play darts, but I was hopeless, and when the wall began to be pockmarked by my darts as they missed the board, Doris suggested we leave it to the men. So we talked about our life in domestic service.

'My last place in service was in a huge house in Belgravia,' said Doris. 'There were twelve servants indoors, as well as two chauffeurs and several gardeners. By this time I was second housemaid and earning £20 a year. It wasn't a bad place at all, except that they were so religious. We were expected to attend church every Sunday, and had our own special pews. The servants' bedrooms were plastered with religious tracts to the effect that "honest toil was no disgrace"; we should "respect our masters"; we should be "sober and diligent". As to the latter, the opportunities to be otherwise were conspicuously lacking. I nearly married the second-gardener in that house. We had been courting on the quiet for some months; we didn't dare be seen, as such human passions as kissing and cuddling were the work of the devil—or so we were told. The under-parlourmaid and I couldn't help wondering how our employers had produced eight children without passion of some kind.

'One day the butler discovered Jack and me kissing goodnight at the back door. By the look on his face you'd have thought we were being highly immoral. I was petrified with fright for Mr Dean, the butler, was a tall, imposing, out-of-this-world individual whom one could never imagine stooping so low as to kiss a female. He was the boss over us, but he wasn't the boss over the outdoor servants. So when, in his church-warden voice, he told my Jack to be off, Jack told him in no uncertain terms where *he* could go. Unfortunately, although Mr Dean had no jurisdiction over gardeners, he could, and did, complain to Madam that Jack was impertinent. Poor Jack got the sack. I think Madam thought that I was imperilling my immortal soul. Still, it was all for the best, for after that I met Joe. He was working in a cycle factory, nothing whatever to do with domestic service.'

'You know, that Joe may be full of book-knowledge, but he's not half as good as me when it comes to playing darts. It took him a dozen throws even to start; he just could not get the double top,' Albert told me, on the way home.

I tactfully refrained from mentioning that Joe's book-learning had got him a good job at almost double Albert's wage. The financial benefits to be accrued from dart-playing were non-existent, consisting merely of free liquid refreshment.

I tried to get Daisy Bumbelow to come to an evening class with me. We were reading poetry then. What a hope. Not only did her Dick flatly refuse to be left at home with the three kids —selfish man—but Daisy herself was of the opinion that poetry wasn't her cup of tea.

'I like limericks, Margaret. Have you heard the one about the young lady from Pinner?'

I hadn't, and when I did, its bawdiness made me realise that Daisy would certainly be an alien element in our poetry class; we were all very earnest. Each week we had to recite a verse from a poem we had liked while at school. My choice was extremely limited as in our school we seemed to have read only three, *The Pied Piper of Hamelin, Lord Ullin's Daughter*, and a funeral dirge about death laying his icy hand on kings. In those days, I had a phenomenal memory, I knew the entire epic of the Pied Piper by heart, so I settled for that. I think some of the students were budding drama aspirants, for they would stand up and declaim a verse using all the appropriate—and inappropriate —expressions like some fifth-rate ham actor. One very formidable lady there struck awe into most of us. She had an enormous bosom on which rested a dainty gold locket. When she stood up, carrying all before her like a ship's figurehead, and gave us an oratorical rendering of *How Horatio kept the Bridge*, with the gold locket rising up and down on her chest like a yo-yo, it was difficult to suppress our mirth.

I invited a male student home one evening for coffee. He was a meek and mild little man with a receding chin and a few straggly ginger hairs. I chose him as a good example to Albert of how completely innocuous were the people that I mixed with. Even Albert could see that there was no comparison between his physical charms and those of this timid little man; any female would have needed to be desperate to take on poor Mr Pratt. I wondered whether I should stir him up; purely from an altruistic point of view, of course. It seemed sad that he should never know what it was all about. But when I suggested this plan to Albert, he thought I would do more harm than good; he was probably right, too.

Mr Pratt lived with his widowed Mother; she 'enjoyed bad health'. I bet she literally enjoyed it too, if only to keep her son dancing attendance on her.

'Mother's only got me now,' Mr Pratt explained. 'All the others are married with families, and live far away.'

I bet they thanked their lucky stars for that, too. I felt really sorry for that poor, ineffectual little man.

'Didn't you ever want to marry, Mr Pratt? And have a family? What will you do when your Mother is gone?'

'Oh! I couldn't leave Mother. I did once bring home a young lady from an evening class, but Mother didn't care for her, said that she wasn't half good enough for me. Though you know, I did rather like her; like you, she was jolly.'

Mr Pratt reminded me of Arthur Scroggins. He rented the floor above us when we lived in Shepherds Bush. Poor Arthur was a very sad and lonely man, about fifty years old. His widowed Mother had died two years ago, and Arthur was lost without her. He would lament to me:

'You know, Mrs Powell, my Mother was the salt of the earth, a saint. I never looked at, or wanted another woman, while Mother and I were together, and now it's too late. I'm all on my own.'

It certainly was too late for poor Arthur. I couldn't imagine any woman wanting to look after him. Almost bald, stooping, with weak watery eyes and a straggly little moustache, he aroused no emotions, either sexual or maternal. But I discovered, later on, his vice.

One morning about seven o'clock, when Albert had gone on his milk-round and the children were still asleep, I was lying comfortably in bed thinking, 'as soon as the sun reaches that black spot on the ceiling, I'll get up', and idly wondering how the spot had suddenly appeared. The next morning, when I looked up, to my surprise, the spot was slightly larger. So, when I was alone I got the step-ladder and climbed up to inspect it. I found that it was a hole Mr Scroggins had bored through his floor and into our bedroom ceiling, so that he could spy on Albert and me in bed. Poor Arthur, he must have had many a fruitless night. What a frustrating task trying to observe the love-life of a milkman who had to be up at 4.30 every morning.

I stuffed the hole with paper, covered it over with white chalk, and never spoke of it to anybody—least of all Albert. I felt so sorry for poor Arthur. He knew I had found out, for when we met on the stairs the following week, he said, 'Thank you.'

Shortly after the birth of our second baby, my parents came up to see us and the child. I was relieved that they had waited for a few weeks, as this baby, unlike my first, resembled at birth nothing so much as a wrinkled red crab-apple. Daisy's child, born a few weeks earlier, was much prettier than mine—I had greatly admired little Nicholas. So when she came up to do the same for mine, I promptly told her, 'Don't bother to drool over him, Daisy, I'm not myopic. Neither am I so overcome with motherly love that I can't see he's no budding Clark Gable.'

I didn't mind that he wasn't pretty. He had a lovely disposition, was so contented and never kept us awake at night.

My Mother, with no experience whatsoever of the difficulties of finding accommodation in London—especially with children—was horrified to see how cramped we were. In her usual forthright and often tactless manner, she proceeded to tell Albert, who was inwardly seething with rage, how impossible it was for me to cook, wash and clean in such a place. Mother was wrong; it wasn't impossible. Plenty of families larger than ours were living quite happily in similar conditions. I tried to change the subject, but Mum would have her say.

'How do you expect Nell to do all the washing? Where will she hang it? and how is she going to get a large pram up and down all these stairs? She can't put a new baby in a folding push-chair. And only one lavatory for twelve people, and that right down in the yard. The landlord should be shown up. It wants reporting to sanitary authorities.'

I was furious with my Mother for Albert's sake. A better husband and Father at looking after his home one could never have. I told Mother this, and only to save my Father grief, did I endeavour to smooth things down by introducing politics, always a red rag to a bull where Mother was concerned.

'Do you know, Nell, we are going to have a Labour Party Conference in Brighton, and your Dad isn't even interested? I never thought the day would dawn when your Father was indifferent to the success or failure of the Labour Party. But remember what I told you. Now that the League of Nations has collapsed—not that it was ever a real deterrent—we shall have a war.'

Dad and I exchanged sympathetic glances, and later on in the day, when Mum had taken the baby out, Dad and I talked. 'I'm not against the Labour Party, Nell. But where are they going? There's Lansbury and his Christian ideals of Government always at loggerheads with Bevin and the T.U.C. Everything is subject to the Party, and the people are mere appendages. What is one to believe now?'

'Never mind, Dad,' Albert consoled him, 'be like me. I never even think about who's in, or out, for they don't make the slightest difference to my milk-round.'

Albert endeared himself to me by being very fond of my Father. They were alike in so many ways. Good-tempered, tolerant and slow to anger. That is why, of course, they were universally liked. The wonder was that each of them loved his wife, so very different in character from him.

Later on, while I was getting our tea, Mum suddenly exclaimed, 'What on earth is that peculiar smell coming up the stairs? I've never smelt anything like it.'

'Oh!' said Albert, smiling maliciously, 'it's only Daisy Bumbelow opening her bedroom door to get the dried haddock for her husband's tea. She keeps it on top of the wardrobe. Says it's the only place where her two cats can't get at it. She leaves it there all night while they are in bed. To counter the smell, she sprinkles the beds in the morning with eau-de-cologne, bought from Woolworth's.'

To see my Mother's face after this recital from Albert was hilarious. She opened her mouth to denounce such appalling goings-on; thought better of it with Albert gazing at her, and relapsed into furious silence.

Mind you, Mum was right. The smell was indescribable. Two adults, four kids now, and the dried haddock all in one small bedroom, with the window shut all night. I once said to Daisy, 'Why don't you and Dick do the same as us—sleep on a bed-settee in the front room and let the children have the bedroom to themselves?'

'Oh, it doesn't matter us all being together. The kids are too young to understand what's going on. Though the other night,' said Daisy, giggling, 'my eldest, Olivia, woke up and asked what Daddy was doing. I told her to go to sleep, Daddy was doing his exercises.'

All her children had been given high-falutin' names. Olivia, Penelope, Violet, and now the new baby, Nicholas. As Daisy said, 'We'll never be able to give the poor b——s a good start; let's give them a decent name and perhaps that will be a help to making it on their own.'

One of the most constant traits of Albert, is his equanimity. Also, although he is no Oscar Wilde when it comes to contributing his quota to light scintillating conversation, he has a strong predilection for uttering irrefutable truths. And as I love to refute, I challenge his statements, and if I am proved wrong, I get extremely irritable. I really hate being proved wrong. But when I have established Albert's argument as fallacious, he is just as sweet-tempered as before. He says he has got all he desires. Me, two kids and a job that he really likes doing.

One drawback to being a milk-roundsman is that the position is static, there is no promotion. Where could you promote to? In theory, you could be moved to a better round, where your customers were wealthier and bought more, thus enabling you to earn more commission. But in actual practice, a roundsman is seldom taken off his usual round. His customers dislike a change and are apt to ring up the depot to say they will change their dairy if their usual milkman goes. Mind you, they ring up for other reasons too. One of Albert's customers regularly rang the depot once a week—the day that Albert asked her to pay the bill—to complain that the milkman had been rude and if he wasn't taken off the round, she would change her dairy. No notice was ever taken of this as all the tradesmen knew what a bad payer she was, and would have refused to serve her. It used to worry me, but never Albert.

'Don't give it a thought, my love. They all know her at the depot. She's permanently soured because her husband went off with a much younger and prettier girl. She tells anybody who will listen, "I gave Mr Reed the best years of my life. Now I'm cast off like an old shoe for some young Jezebel. May he get the pox from her." I'd disappear too, Margaret, right quick, if I had to look at that face across the breakfast table.'

There's no getting away from it, having a pretty face means you start life with a great natural advantage. You've already half-way got it made. If the façade is admirable, people don't enquire too closely about the value of the interior. I remember my school friend Ursula, antipathetic to discipline, at the end of the queue when brains were dished out, but getting away with murder because she was attractive. Even teachers prefer to gaze at a pretty face, rather than an earnest plain Jane. As I couldn't shine in school through my physical attributes, I simply had to be clever. I have recently given a farewell speech at my old, and only, school, now due to be demolished after 97 years. I started there at three and a half years old and left at thirteen. I had my day of fame there too, my brief moment of glory. Even now my memory is fairly good, but at that time it was exceptional. One day, in front of the class I recited the whole seemingly interminable poem, *The Pied Piper of Hamelin*. Nothing would deter me from going on and on, although I could sense the class were bored to tears. When I reached the lines 'Rats! they fought the dogs and killed the cats,' I declaimed 'Rats' in a loud and histrionic voice, and a girl in the front row muttered, sotto voce,

'Rats to you too.' But I didn't let such jealousy throw me off my stride. I was somebody at last.

Albert delivered milk to two young and pretty girls who shared a basement flat. One of them, Valerie, was a painter, though not a very successful one. Along with the milk, Albert dispensed sympathy when Valerie couldn't sell a picture, and felicitations when she did. Her most successful efforts were what she called her bread and butter pictures of cats and dogs. There are always people ready to go into transports of love over animals —their own, or just animals in general. But the pictures that Valerie treasured—and very occasionally found a buyer for— were great swirling masses of colour that seemed to shift and change before your very eyes. I'm sure that they were good paintings, but personally I wouldn't have wanted one in my home. Somehow they made one feel uncomfortable. The day that Valerie sold one of these for £20 was certainly an event. She invited us both over in the evening to a wine party. I must admit that Albert and I were somewhat out of our element in such arty company. Nevertheless it gave me the idea that perhaps I could paint if only I acquired the basic knowledge. Why, I too might sell a picture. Immediately my imagination conjured up delectable visions of my name in the paper, one-man exhibitions and greatly increased standard of living for Albert and me. Albert thought it a good idea. But then he mostly did think that my ideas, however outlandish or far-fetched, were good, as naturally he was predisposed in my favour.

I suggested to Stan's wife—she was still keeping up her afternoon class—that we both sign on for a course in painting; the cost was only 7/6 per term, and we supplied our own materials. There were about sixteen in the class, of whom three or four were like us, absolute beginners. I wondered if I was about to discover that I had a hidden talent for artistic expression. If I had, it remained hidden. I think our teacher realised, even quicker than I did, that I had no aptitude, natural or otherwise. But as it was no part of his job to discourage effort, however misguided, he refrained from saying this until I asked his honest opinion. However, I did have the pleasure of finding that my friend, Alice, had a very good eye for colour and perspective.

She never became proficient enough to sell her landscapes, but hung them all over the house, much to the mortification of Stanley, who although delighted with his wife's metamorphosis in appearance since I had worked on her, had no desire to find she had talents denied to him.

Albert was, as usual, very sympathetic over my failure, and took me out for the evening. He was always there to meet me at the end of every term, either to buy drinks to celebrate that I had passed, or drinks to console me for failure. He was indeed my 'Rock of Gibraltar'.

Chapter 7

I hesitated for some considerable time before telling Albert that there was going to be yet another addition to our family. I knew that he would be far from pleased as he considered, with good cause, that even two children were more than we could afford to keep.

In trying to prevent the third child from appearing I took so much medicine that I nearly disappeared myself. But nothing happened. Even if I had had the money, and had known of a person who did abortions, nothing on earth would have induced me to resort to those lengths. I felt particularly to blame for having a third child, because after the second, I had been to the birth-control clinic, recently set up in Ladbroke Grove. I certainly felt guilty going there. A lot of us mothers did, strange as it may seem. We felt that it was almost as reprehensible to prevent having children, as to abort them. It was all tied up with the deeply ingrained principle that it wasn't moral to have the pleasures without the pains.

It was my fault that a third child was on the way. Albert relied on me as, used properly, the method was very reliable. Its one drawback was that its effectiveness did require you to know whether you were going to need it that particular night. If one were in the habit of frequently making love, fine, a woman could put up with the slight discomfort of perpetually wearing the preventative. But if its use was only occasional, one was never prepared. And by the time you discovered you needed it, that was the deathknell to the spontaneous love act. So one took a chance, as I had, and lost.

By the time it became inevitable that Albert should know he was once again to experience the inestimable joy of becoming a father, I decided that attack was the best form of defence. I would be indignant and aggrieved about the inconvenience of having another baby.

'Why should it always be me, Albert, who has to take precautions? If you don't bother, why should I? It's a mutual operation, isn't it? Anyway, it's me who's got to have it and endure all the extra work. And you can't give me any more money, so what have you got to lose? Besides, it might be a girl. You'll love having a daughter.'

Poor Albert, he contemplated with dismay the months of me and my unsatisfied fads and fancies. He worked so hard that to come home to an emotional pregnant wife wasn't exactly welcome.

'One thing I do know, Margaret. We will have to move from these rooms. To have yet another baby born up here, with all the work and washing it entails, is not to be thought of. We'll try for rooms on a ground floor. Come to that, I won't be sorry to leave here, and get away from those Bumbelows. Their kids make the place a Bedlam, especially that Violet who never seems to leave off bawling.'

What a heart-breaking job it was looking for somewhere to live with two children and another on the way. We must have inspected dozens of rooms. Some were so damp that moss was growing on the walls, in others the floors had sunk, so that everything was on the slant. Yet others, in dark dungeon-like basements, seemed to exude a sinister aura of poverty and cruelty. I shuddered to think of having to live there myself, let alone bring up children. Eventually we managed to rent three rooms on the ground floor of a three-storey house. As usual there was no bathroom or hot water, one lavatory and that in the yard; with so many people using it, it needed to be. The landlady lived at a considerable distance from the house, fortunately. If possible, we would never take rooms where the owners lived in the house. They would be everlastingly complaining about the children: about their making too much noise, kicking the paint about or some other crime. In fact, by the time I had three children, it often seemed to me that having them was a crime in itself.

As a rule, Albert would never get too friendly with the other tenants, saying, with some justification, that as we had to live in such close proximity, it was bad policy to encourage even closer contact. But during our time in this house, Albert got very friendly with the family on the floor above us, a Mr and Mrs Delauney and their two children. I used to get really annoyed at his frequent trips up the stairs. Not jealous, because I suffered no apprehensions that it was Mrs Delauney's charms that lured Albert up there, I knew it was Jack Delauney's conversation. I liked Angela Delauney in spite of her conversation being so liberally peppered with swear words. At least, unlike Mr Delauney, she never pretended to be other than what she was. Albert considered that she was as 'common as dirt'.

'You know,' Albert would too often tell me, 'I feel sorry for Jack. He has been a somebody. You can tell by his cultured voice that he came from a good family. He was telling me only the other day that he can trace his pedigree back to the Normans; Delauney is an old French name. He deserves something better than that slatternly Angela. She would drag any man down. No wonder they quarrel so violently. Why, Jack was telling me that he never can keep a job for long because that awful wife of his comes round to where he works and raises hell by asking to see his employer. She wants to know just what her husband earns and what hours he works. Can you imagine how mortifying that must be for Jack?'

I used to get infuriated at hearing all this guff. 'The man's a phoney. However can you be taken in by such a walking tailor's dummy? Can't you sense that his so-called cultured voice is only a thin veneer overlaying his working-class origins? As for tracing his ancestry back to the Normans, don't make me laugh. I wouldn't mind betting he doesn't even know his own grandfather. The man's probably been a butler or valet and copies the way they speak upstairs. For heaven's sake don't think he is superior to you, Albert, you could knock spots off him for looks and brains. *And* you look after the home, which is more than Mr Delauney does; he likes neither his wife nor his children. The only thing he cares about is that smelly dog that he says is worth pounds.'

These remarks, while highly gratifying to Albert's ego, did

nothing to change his opinion of that 'Norman Conqueror'.

Occasionally, while Mr Delauney was at work, I would go up and have a cup of tea with Angela; though I often shuddered inwardly at the amount of germs I might be swallowing, and I'd never eat anything. Once Angela dropped a piece of cake on the floor and it collected a layer of dirt. 'Ah, well,' said Angela airily, as she flicked the muck off, 'my Mum always said you have to eat a peck of bloody dirt before you die.' Not all at once, was my thought. As far as I could see, the only one in that home who had a pedigree was the dog. Angela's origins were mercifully shrouded in mystery. Though, from what Mr Delauney called her in their frequent rows, her parentage was somewhat purple and bastard. Angela, knowing that he couldn't be outdone in the matter of choice adjectives, always retaliated with a lurid description of Jack's sexual prowess—or lack of it—which she likened to a bloody puff of wind; there one minute, gone the next. And she added, for good measure, that as for bastardy, he needn't look any further than his own kids. Whether there was any truth in this statement I never knew for sure, but Jack Delauney would never pursue it. Perhaps he would not admit, even to himself, that he had not fathered his children. He certainly would never have admitted to the ignominy of being impotent.

Once, when Angela was in a more than usually expansive mood, she hinted that the eldest child, a rather handsome boy who bore no resemblance to her husband, was the progeny of the milkman, a way of working off the bill. When I told Albert this he was extremely indignant at this slur upon his calling. 'No milkman that I have ever known, and that includes me, would want to do that to a woman like her. Besides, no milkman could ever stay long enough at the house.'

'For heaven's sake, Albert, how long does the job take? It's all over before you can say Jack Robinson.'

'Anyway,' added Albert, 'I still say that no self-respecting milkman would want to be frivolous with that woman. Not unless he was blind and had lost his sense of smell.'

How awful can men get? They really believe that they are doing a woman a great favour by going to bed with them. Besides, I don't suppose Angela was always as blowsy and un-

89

washed. I liked to listen to her descriptions of the running battles she had with social workers.

'They get a foot in your door, and in five bloody minutes they have made a catalogue of your home. The fact that you haven't made the bloody beds, that there are no sheets or pillow-cases. They ask you if you've got mice—who hasn't—and how do you manage for a bath. I told her, we wash down as far as possible and up as far as possible, and as the middle bit is no bloody use we don't bother about it. You should have seen her face, Margaret. She was about fifty, and I'm bloody sure she thought kids dropped from heaven. She even had the bloody nerve to say I shouldn't smoke so much; it was bad for me, I'd do better by spending the money on food. Bloody hell! I told her: shoot that b—— who shares my bed and I'll give up the fags.'

As it happened, before long Angela did get rid of her Jack, though not in the way she had suggested. I very much disliked Jack Delauney. More than that, I felt a kind of repulsion when-ever he came near me. I loathed his fat, round, smooth and shiny face on which no wrinkles showed. His small eyes and sparse eyebrows, his sleek and unctuous manner made me shud-der. I felt that there was something unhealthy about him. So I was not greatly astonished one morning to see the police going upstairs. Jack Delauney was arrested for interfering with little boys. With great magnanimity I forbore to say 'I told you so' to Albert. He made excuses for that nauseating man.

'What can you expect with a wife like that. Always nagging him about being no good in bed, losing him jobs and never coming home to a clean place. Any man who wasn't a saint would go off the rails.'

What did surprise me was Angela's attitude. She seemed stun-ned by this disclosure of her husband's aberration. She kept on and on about it to me.

'I never thought he was like that, Margaret. I had no idea. I've never seen a sign of it in this place. Whatever will the kids think? They're bound to hear about it at school. I'll never be able to show my face in the street. Whatever are they saying in the local?'

They were not saying much at all in the local. In this district of large families crowded into two or three rooms, struggling for survival with poor wages and unemployment, people were very tolerant of the failures and misfits. Their philosophy was, 'It could have been me. It's the life that does it. What's the good of putting him in prison?'

The young couple on the top floor, Brian and Barbara Mathews, were exceedingly pleasant and charming. They had been married five years and still had no children, a noteworthy event in itself. But in fact, or so they said, they were so much in love with each other that they needed nothing to complement their life.

They both worked, together if possible, and were in and out of jobs with such frequency that their finances were always in a parlous state.

But, unlike Mr Micawber with his 'income twenty pounds, expenditure twenty pounds and sixpence, result misery', they were never miserable. Many and marvellous were the schemes that they concocted, all of which were going to make their fortune. But somehow they all failed. Mr Mathews had received a very good education. The only good it did him, in his opinion, was to leave him with his 'public school' voice, which was a great asset when it came to persuading banks to loan money for another of his 'certain to succeed' ideas. To us, who couldn't have borrowed £5 from anybody, it seemed as though banks were benevolent institutions with unlimited trust in the essential probity of human nature, *if* you had been to the right school.

Brian and I had many friendly arguments over the status of the sexes, Brian contending that men must of necessity be superior to women because their brains were four ounces heavier. I retorted that the brain of Neanderthal man was even heavier, and look what happened to him. Furthermore, doctors had proved that a large part of the brain was never active; that was the extra that men had. One day Barbara came down to us full of excitement over Brian's latest plan. 'We are going round to all the junk shops and markets picking up bargains—Brian knows a lot about antiques—so we can start up a business of our own. We have already found an empty shop. We are going to call our shop "Yours, with love". We'll encourage people to come in and browse around, handle any object they fancy, and we will never pester them to buy. In fact, Brian says we shall hate parting with our things.'

They needn't have worried about the wrench of parting, they very seldom had to face it. 'Theirs' the things remained, permanently, never becoming 'Yours'. As Barbara was a very pretty girl, love came into the shop in abundance, but unfortunately it paid no dividends. After a couple of months they cut their losses and disposed of 'Yours' without love, to a junk man. They were in no way dismayed at this failure. As Brian philosophised, 'Nothing venture, nothing win.'

On another occasion, they took over a moribund business called 'Gentle Cleaning', and personally wrote out cards advertising that the most delicate fabrics could be cleaned safely by this new method. They distributed these cards far and wide through the letter boxes.

Albert said, 'Take my best suit to them, Margaret. If ever anything needed gentle cleaning, that does. The material is so thin it's like wearing tissue paper. I'll be their first customer, give them heart.'

First Albert was, but unfortunately, very few followed him—which didn't surprise me. Oh! the cleaning was gentle enough; the trouble was, it didn't remove the dirt. So that business folded up. Over a cup of tea I expostulated with Brian. 'Don't you know enough about any one subject to make a living at it? Couldn't you be a salesman, or work in an office, or be a teacher? Surely your expensive education has done something for you!'

'Margaret, I know a bit of history and a smattering of chemistry, I can speak French and some Italian. Can you think of a job in which those talents could be put to a lucrative use? If so, let me know and I'll be after it like a bolt from the blue. In the meantime, Barbara and I have got another idea. We are going to make lampshades up in our rooms and sell them direct to the stores.'

Eventually they emigrated to Australia, where, so Barbara reckoned, there was far more scope for Brian's ingenuity in a land of promise with no hide-bound traditions.

Chapter 8

By 1938, a great many people were convinced that a war was inevitable. My Mother, entrenched in her position of one whose prognostications of doom were now coming true, proceeded to verbally lambast 'this government of appeasement'.

'What are they doing I'd like to know? Nothing at all. They've seen Japan invade China, Italy invade Abyssinia, and Hitler march into Austria! And still they act as though some miraculous wind will blow the whole trouble away. Chamberlain and Halifax are the worst, absolutely inept.'

The churches began to have much larger congregations, always a sure sign that people were apprehensive that their departure to the hereafter might occur considerably earlier than they had anticipated. It's a good policy to take out spiritual insurance on such an event. Others with wealth, ever mindful that it is easier for them to go through the eye of a needle than to enter the kingdom of heaven with their money, began to spend this wealth lavishly. But, also mindful that charity begins at home, very little of their money was siphoned in our direction.

My timid and earnest friend, Mr Pratt—whose first name was Cuthbert—had joined me in an evening class on the Russian Classics. We both felt that it gave us a certain cachet to be studying such high-class literature. Mr Pratt had also joined Frank Buchman's Moral Rearmament. He tried to recruit Albert into the Group, with conspicuous lack of success. Albert had never even heard of the movement, and when I explained it to him, he remained unimpressed. Mr Pratt was full of fervour for Frank Buchman—'our leader'. Well, with an over-powering Mother like his, there was little else for his emotions to fasten on. He came back from one weekend with the Group, almost transformed with the spiritual and moral benefits he had derived from associating with them. He related to Albert, at great and detailed length, just how the Group fostered the desirable attributes of unselfishness and strength without violence. As Albert was of the opinion that his character always displayed these admirable traits, Mr Pratt's eloquence fell on deaf ears; while as regards making the slightest difference to the prevention of war, the Group was just as ineffective as the League.

When war became imminent, and thousands of children were being evacuated from London, Albert insisted that I and our family should go down to Hove. We couldn't contemplate parting from the children, mainly because we felt sure they would be split up. No one family would want to take in three brothers. Mrs Briggs had already sent Theodore to the country. Angela Delauney was now living on Public Assistance since, when Jack Delauney came out of prison, he had completely disappeared. In spite of his predilection for little boys, and their once frequent rows, Angela would really have been pleased if he had come back to her. She decided to be evacuated with her children, for, as she explained, 'One place is very much like another when you have no husband and two kids and are living on Public Assistance.'

Though I say it myself, and naturally I always say it myself, my three boys were nice children, well-behaved and well-mannered. So I lived with my sister Pat, who was an absolute heroine to have us all—and Albert too on Sundays—for six months. During that time, while her husband or our Mother minded her and my kids, we learnt Old Time Dancing. Hilarious times we had whilst learning. Once we had mastered the steps, it was never quite so enjoyable.

All my Mother's maternal instincts came to the fore. In the First World War she had had my Father to protect; now she had three sons to worry about. The youngest, Donald who was in the Territorials, had already been called-up; very much to my grief as he was my favourite brother, and, in his khaki uniform, seemed so frail and vulnerable. What did Donald know of war and killing somebody that he had never met and couldn't possibly hate? Somebody who was like him perhaps, who loved people and life, and hoped to marry and have children? Donald

94

had never hated anybody in all his eighteen years; he didn't even know how to, let alone have any idea of killing. Mother regarded anything that disrupted her family as a personal vendetta against herself. She had been warned by Dad and us that no letters about the conduct of the war were to be sent to the War Office. Mum might be the better strategist at deploying her family, but let the generals take over when it came to martial manoeuvres, we told her.

I'd only been in Hove a month when, with the reorganising of the milk-rounds, Albert found he had lost his job. As the man with the longest service there, he never should have been pushed out, but he and the manager were always at logger-heads—afterwards it was discovered that the manager had a criminal record. Albert got a job as a porter, extremely ill-paid, but lost that after a few months because he wasn't on duty when he should have been. He had deserted his post through curiosity, because in the pub over the road was their Saturday 'turn'— a tattooed man. Dressed in only a pair of briefs, tattooed on every inch of his skin in glowing colours, he was, said Albert, an incredible kaleidoscopic sight as he twisted and turned in a sort of dance.

After the false alarm of the air-raid siren on the day we declared war, nothing at all happened. So after six months, I was determined to return to London and Albert. When he could not talk me out of returning, Albert went to the head office of the Express Dairy to see if they could fix him up somewhere. They agreed that he never should have had to leave his round; but the best they could do in the circumstances was to fit him up with a round near Bromley. At first I couldn't bear the place; it seemed a nowhere habitation, neither city, country nor seaside. Albert too, was sorry to leave his old district where so many of his customers had been his friends, for Albert was such a cheerful and obliging milkman, always ready with a joke, even in the rain or snow. His customers had really looked forward to his second-round call. He did odd jobs: put on new tap washers, repaired fuses, even mended their alarm-clocks. They consulted him as to where they should go for their holidays, and what they should do for little Bobby's cough. He consoled them when they became pregnant yet again; unfortunately, Albert knew of no panacea for unwanted babies. He served the rich and poor, unknown and famous. One of the famous ones was George Arliss, the film star—whatever part he played, he always seemed to be George Arliss. He may have had money but he never distributed any of it among the tradesmen, not even at Christmas. This parsimony so incensed the dustmen that they used to leave a trail of rubbish along his garden path. Very different was Archie de Bear—Albert said he was something to do with entertainment. He always told Albert, 'Now don't forget to let me know when you are going on a holiday, you will need some pourboire.' Then there was Robb Wilton, the music-hall comedian. If ever he tried any of his jokes on Albert, it must have been a depressing experience. Albert is not given to falling about with laughter.

I suppose it was around August 1940 that the air-raids started to become a regular nightly occurrence. By this time we had managed to get a council house on the Downham estate near Lewisham. We all had Anderson shelters in the garden, and as the raids increased in ferocity and duration, nobody even started the evening indoors—we all went straight to the shelters to sleep. During one phase we spent fifty-seven consecutive nights in our shelter to the accompaniment of the whine and roar of exploding bombs and the whistle and scream of the ack-ack. Albert was an absolute tower of strength in all this time. There we were, in the semi-darkness of the Anderson, the children asleep, me silent with terror, and Albert blithely totting up his day's takings, for all the world as though he was sitting in an armchair in the house. It wasn't that he was putting on an act for my edification. Albert literally didn't know what fear was.

Every day, as I shopped, took the children to school and collected them later, I passed horrible and grim evidence of the havoc of the night, houses smashed to pieces, or in some cases just the front collapsed, disclosing, as it were, the entire private life of the family who had lived there. This invasion of their privacy seemed somehow more terrible, and almost obscene, than did the debris of homes, shops and broken water-mains. The incendiary bombs had devastated London. At dawn one morning, as I stood in my garden, gazing towards the heart of London, it appeared to be ringed in fire. The acrid smell of burning was in the air and the sky for miles around held a ruddy glow. Inevitably, I thought of that other Great Fire of London, not to be compared with this modern one in terms of human suffering. The tragedies became more personal as people one actually knew, had spoken to perhaps the day before, but now would never speak to again, were killed by bombs. The wife and five children of the happiest family I had known, after spending two cold hours in their shelter one midday, came out thinking it was all-clear and were all killed as a stick of bombs fell at the end of our road. Hundreds of us packed into the church for the funeral service. I received no feeling of consolation; what the bereaved, and almost demented husband and father felt, I could not imagine. To me, the church is always in a dilemma. In wartime, it needs to follow the precepts of the Old Testament, total destruction to your enemies. In peace, then the New Testament is the way of life. How do you convey to a man bereft of all that made life worth living, that it is the 'will of God', that we cannot fathom His unknown and unseen purpose, and that they have all gone to heaven to wait for him? It merely increases the agony, as who would want to know their loved ones are at the whim of such an arbitrary deity? Who can see a divine purpose in the killing of children?

Suddenly, for a while, the air-raids ceased, and once again we could sleep in our beds. During this time, in September 1941, Albert got his call-up papers, and I determined that once he had gone, it would be pointless to stay in London. I wrote to Mother to ask her to keep an eye open for an empty house in Hove.

The four years that Albert spent in the Air Force didn't have the slightest effect on the duration or conduct of the war. In fact, it often seemed as though only I and the Post Office where I drew my allotment were aware of Albert's existence. He was thirty-eight before his country decided that his assistance was necessary to the winning of the war. I gave him explicit instructions that not only was he to be a reluctant hero, it would be politic to be no kind of hero at all. I quoted to him from Kipling, the same as my Mother did to Dad before he departed for France in the First World War—Mum was a Kipling fan—

97

'It's Tommy this, an' Tommy that, an' "Chuck him out, the brute!" But it's "Saviour of 'is country" when the guns begin to shoot.'

Not that I needed to worry; Albert had never had any intention of putting himself in a position of hazard if he could possibly avoid it. He was already imbued with the idea of making his service life 'a piece of cake'. Albert explained this philosophy to me the night before he left for Cardington. 'You see, Margaret, it's all an attitude of mind. If I go into the Air Force full of worry and anxiety about you, the kids, what's going to happen to us when the war is over, then I shan't enjoy the job.'

'But Albert, you aren't supposed to enjoy it. You are doing your duty and duty is seldom enjoyable. Besides, I'm sure you are more use serving milk and goods every day, than you will be where you are going.'

But Albert really knew that I wasn't sorry to see him finish in Downham. The hard work of doing almost two rounds in one, the worry of the ration coupons, the nagging of some of his customers who were convinced that Albert let Mrs So-and-So have more rations than she was entitled to, had turned Albert from a happy and easy-going person into a morose man who snapped at me and the children on the slightest provocation. Not only for our sakes did I not mind his leaving, it was for him as well. And at his age, thirty-eight, with no experience whatever of flying, I knew that he wouldn't be sent on any bombing expeditions. In fact, he wasn't even in an air-raid.

Chapter 9

Albert chose the RAF partly because he liked the uniform; he thought that it looked less itchy than khaki. Even if the Royal Navy would have taken him, Albert couldn't see himself in bell-bottoms, and as for the Merchant Navy, it would have been even more difficult for the convoys to get through if Albert had been one of the crew.

The first questions he was asked at the recruitment centre in Lewisham were, 'What can you do? Have you any mechanical knowledge?'

The only mechanical knowledge Albert had was that needed for the constant repairing of his ancient rusty bicycle. The recruitment officer's opinion was that the ability to mend punctures and bicycle chains would hardly qualify him as an expert at 'keeping the planes in the air'. Neither did he think that there were any milk-rounds in the service, though when he heard that Albert had been a butcher, he said, 'What about going in the cookhouse?' Why should an ability to cut up meat also mean that you knew how to cook it? Certainly Albert didn't at that time.

Eventually, in despair, the officer suggested the Military Police. As Albert wrote to me later on, 'I ought to have been suspicious, as, apart from my height, I had no qualifications for being a policeman.'

Albert didn't realise that it meant he would have no friends, except other Military Police.

I gave a fond farewell to Albert at the railway station—though not as fond as one of his sisters. She was weeping copiously, and I believe, was rather shocked at my being dry-eyed. But then, I had been brought up in a home where public displays of emotion were frowned upon. Furthermore, our marriage wasn't, and never had been, highly over-charged, neither had I wanted it to be. My previous experiences of falling in love had induced such painful sensations, such pangs of jealousy and despair, such intermittent feelings of bliss and enchantment, all ending in pathetic and tear-laden recriminations, that I determined never again to become so vulnerable. What Albert and I had, and still have, was a deep affection and understanding.

Albert wrote to me from Cardington. 'You should have seen the carriage full of potential airmen, you'd have died of laughing. When I surveyed the motley collection of males around me, I could well understand why the Government had waited so long before calling us up, and how desperate a situation England must be in. If Hitler could have seen this new batch of recruits, he would have thought the war as good as won. There we were, all around forty years old, fat, thin, short and tall, all wanting to be grounded airmen and never to bring ourselves to the notice of the C.O. There was a bus to take us from the station to Cardington. Until we reached the camp we had been laughing and lolling around as we pleased. But as soon as those massive iron gates clanged behind us, our lives altered. We had to stand rigidly to attention, and then march to our hut. I tell you, Margaret, that was when we realised that we were no longer free men. We were handed a cup of muddy-looking cocoa, which tasted foul. One of the fellows reckoned it had bromide in, to dampen our sexual impulses. As far as I can tell from this camp, there is little to arouse them. We had another medical, with complete lack of privacy. The sight of twenty-four men, some who obviously hadn't taken any exercise in years, standing there with their trousers around their ankles, was ludicrous in the extreme. One poor devil with bulging nipples blushed fiery red when the M.O. said, "God, what sex are you? Are you sure it's not the WAAF camp you want?"

'I'm no Clark Gable but in comparison with some here with their protruding stomachs, flat feet and varicose veins, I feel you are lucky to have me. Even though you haven't got me at the moment, I'm worth waiting for.'

The colossal egoism of the male sex never ceases to amaze me. The letter continued, 'I'm graded A1, and when I asked the M.O. why, as I weighed under nine stone, he replied, with a cynical grin, "You'll be just the right size for cleaning out sewage pipes." We have been issued with our uniforms; mine fits where it touches, which it doesn't in many places. The fellows with money have already taken their uniforms into town and had them altered. I'm not sorry we are to be here only eight days. We are crammed into a hut and some of the men have never heard of fresh air. You were always complaining about my feet. You should be here. The smell is indescribable, a combination of ripe Stilton and Gorgonzola. If there was a gas attack, we'd never be able to smell it.'

This nice, loving and sentimental letter cheered me considerably. I could tell that Albert wasn't too heartbroken at missing his home comforts, edible and otherwise. In all the four years of Albert's service, I never did get a letter devoted to love and the pangs of separation. He told me, though I find it hard to believe, that he did write such letters, but they were so heavily censored that it wasn't worth posting them.

I was now making arrangements to move our home down to Hove. My next-door neighbour, a strict evangelical church-going spinster of no charms whatsoever inflicted on me a long discourse on the perils of a place like Brighton, especially in wartime. 'All those men in the forces, away from their wives, are just waiting to take advantage of a woman whose husband is absent.' So often have I found that elderly unmarried females seem to have the most erotic and prurient idea as to what constitutes married life. They must imagine that sex and bed account for three parts of it. People like Miss Bell, who could seldom, if ever have had the opportunity to leave the path of righteousness, are very often prone to uttering moral diatribes.

I was happy to be back in my home town, even although now the sea-front was embellished with coils of barbed wire. Hove at that time was very lively, as the 4th Division of the British Columbia regiment were billeted in large empty houses in the town. The pubs were doing a roaring trade, for the Canadians had plenty of money. Their rate of pay, like the Americans', was considerably higher than that of a British soldier. They had all been issued with a booklet on how to treat the indigenous population, and warned not to act as though they had temporarily taken over our country. Judging by the occasional bar-brawls, some of them hadn't bothered to read the booklet.

Somewhat to my surprise, Albert's next letter was still very cheerful. I had thought that by now, without me, his life would resemble an arid desert. Well, it should have done so. In reality, when the war was over, and things had settled down to some degree of normality, Albert greatly missed the life. He has frequently told me, with absolute truth but also, I cannot help feeling, a certain lack of tact, that his four years in the forces were the very best years of his life. He had a marvellous time.

He wrote, 'We have now been sent to Bridlington to do our square-bashing; our "civvies" will be sent home. We are billeted in empty houses near the sea-front. I share a room with a bank clerk, a solicitor and a very lively cockney we call "Dive-Bomber Jones". He's got that name because he is hopeless on the firing range. After the "cease fire" there's always one more shot. That's Dive-Bomber Jones—we all dive for cover. Harold, the solicitor, is another laugh. He wouldn't send home his bowler hat, said it would ruin it. Varied and obscene are the remarks he gets about this hat; from putting it under the bed to using it for a purpose I cannot write down. He wears it when we go over to the showers "to protect his head", he says. The showers are certainly a hazardous affair. The water starts off tepid and then without warning gushes out like a boiling Niagara. Some mornings nothing, no water at all, and we go back as smelly as when we entered. Believe me, we sweat here. Yesterday, we had a twelve-mile route march. We have to carry a pack that's absolutely square. It doesn't matter what's in it, some put bricks in to make the squareness. I've already got a pal in the cookhouse. He gave me some empty square mess-tins, much lighter than bricks. I'm used to walking, so I managed all right. It was a nightmare to our bank clerk, Len. As we struggled back, Len cursing the war, the Air Force and the corporal in charge, he looked at the line of men and muttered, "It's worse than the bloody retreat from Moscow." I expect you know what he meant, my love. Directly we got back, came the order, "five minutes to change for P.T." You should have seen the pandemonium and heard the language. "Effing bloody lot of crabs," from the

Dive-Bomber, and from Harold, "It's worse than Torquemada" —whoever *he* is. Probably you know. That's the worst of being billeted with two cultured blokes, I don't understand half of what they say. Good job me and Dive-Bomber understand each other.

'We had to trot down to the sea front for P.T. all wearing white shorts and singlets. In the rush, Len, who refused to wear regulation pants, had forgotten to remove his highly-coloured ones, which showed below the shorts. You should have heard our corporal bawl out, "Step out that monster from outer space, that prissy purple-legs." Poor old Len, and all the public looking on. There were a couple of men standing by the fence behind me, and one murmured, "There is a corner of a foreign field that is forever England. And looking at this lot I wish I was there." Anyway, not to worry, I'm doing fine. I have a pal in the cookhouse who feeds me, and a pal in the stores who has got me a pair of shoes.'

I read most of this out to the children, in case they were beginning to forget that they had a father. David, who was then eight, was quiet for a moment, and then said, 'When is Dad going to drop bombs on the Germans? Why did he go to the war if he isn't going in an aeroplane?'

I explained that Dad's job was to 'keep them flying'. Actually in all his four years' service Albert saw only one plane on the ground. What a waste of his time.

My Mother was a frequent visitor. She much preferred to come to see me rather than have my three boys leaving dirty marks in her house. Dad would sometimes manage to see me without her; I greatly valued his company, even though we were both so inarticulate with each other. Mother hated all wars, and this one more than most. It had already deprived her of the company of her three sons; two were in the forces and one in the fire service. With the advent of the United States and Russia which transformed a European into a World War, my Mother, normally indifferent to matters of religion, was convinced that Armageddon was nigh. Once, when my friend Vi—an evacuee from London—was having a cup of tea with me, my Mother called in. She didn't take to Vi at all because of her colourful language; every other word seemed to be a 'b' or an 'f'. But, as

Mother was full of rage and grief, because she had no news of her youngest son, she couldn't wait until Vi had gone.

'It all follows from the faithlessness of statesmen and politicians, from rejecting the precepts of the League to disarm. They all paid lip-service to the necessity for disarmament while all were determined that they wouldn't be the first to start. What this country needs is pacifists, men like Gandhi, who don't believe in violence.'

Here, much to Mum's discomfiture, Vi burst out laughing. 'You mean that funny bald little man who trots around wearing only a loin-cloth. It would be a bit comical if we had a few walking around here dressed like that.'

As Vi's only other knowledge of India consisted of the Black Hole of Calcutta, the conversation—or rather monologue—from my Mother abruptly ceased.

When next I heard from Albert, he was in the sick bay—though, judging by the tone of the letter, not suffering unduly. Most of the letter was taken up with his daily routine and how he got into the sick bay.

'Every morning we have gun-drill. It's enough to make a good soldier lay down his arms and surrender. For guns we use broomsticks. You should have heard Dive-Bomber Jones when we got issued with them.

' "Gor Blimey, I didn't know I had joined the effing boy scouts. Gawd, what would me old dutch say if she could see me with this effing broom-stick. She'd bloody well tell me where I could put it."

'I must say, Margaret, we did look a bit like a Fred Karno's army. Mind you, I was glad they weren't real guns as none of us had an idea how to carry a gun, slope or shoulder arms. One poor chap got so tangled up with his broomstick that he tripped over it and fell headlong—much to the amusement of the general public. If he'd been let loose among them, he'd have gone berserk.

'After we had mastered gun-drill—still using broomsticks for guns—we had another exercise to do. I'll try to explain it. We formed into pairs, and one had to lie rigid on his back on the ground, while the other tried to turn him over on to his face. I know it sounds easy, but it isn't. When Dive-Bomber Jones saw the size of his partner, he bawled out, "Hi corporal, I haven't joined up to be a bloody coal-heaver. Blimey, I'm going home, while I've still got enough energy for me old dutch." My partner was Harold, the solicitor. I thought he would be a soft touch doing that kind of work. Afterwards, I found out he played squash rackets twice a week. In trying to be nonchalant and look as though the job was a piece of cake, I ricked my back and the pain nearly crippled me. While the others were doubling back to camp, I limped along bent double, causing much hilarity to a couple of WAAFs. Passing out parade is in two weeks' time. I've got to be fit by then. Bomber's just been in to see me. He reckons I'm better at skrimshanking than he is. That's praise indeed.'

The paucity of the separation allowance made me decide to get a daily job, at tenpence an hour, about 4p now. I shared this job with another daily, a Mrs Gates; we each did three mornings. Poor Mrs Gates had a very hard life with a husband who was shell-shocked in the First World War, when he was only twenty. He now suffered from neurasthenia and was convinced that nobody loved him. Mrs Gates warned me about our employers, and the dangers of getting too friendly with either of them.

'If you do, you'll find that Mrs Whitmore will fasten on you like a limpet, and relate with profuse detail all the iniquities of Mr Whitmore.'

She was right too. Mrs Whitmore was about forty. Somewhat passée although one could still discern traces of her original prettiness. She had a photograph prominently displayed of herself at twenty acting in an amateur production of the Mikado. It's always a mistake to leave evidence around of how you used to look. The contrast is so marked. Mr Whitmore had some kind of Government job, that kept him out of the forces. He had a ravaged, hungry, yet somehow feminine appearance, as though fate had given him a raw deal and he couldn't fathom why. When they were together they sniffed and circled around each other like two cats on heat; yet whenever she touched him he drew back in repulsion.

One morning when I arrived she was shedding copious tears.

I could only be sympathetic, though tears did nothing to enhance her faded charms.

'It's all the fault of Lawrence,' she sobbed. 'He never wants me near him, especially at night. We even have separate beds. I've almost forgotten what sex is like. I might as well be married to a eunuch for all I ever experience. It must be six months since we made love. He looks at me as though I was some kind of object, scarcely human.'

'Perhaps he *has* become a eunuch,' I told her. Naturally I meant it as a joke, but she really took it literally, for, with a horrified expression she screeched, 'Oh, no! It can't be, do you really think so. How could he have lost it?'

I laughed until I too was weeping.

What Esmeralda didn't understand was, that Lawrence wasn't seeing her as a man does a woman, but as a woman does another woman. Although he was a man, and capable of performing a man's functions—as indeed he had done for years—the feminine side of his nature was now uppermost; he was alternately attracted and revolted by his wife. Perhaps the exigencies of the war, the foulness and carnage, had brought to the fore his femaleness, and he was under no necessity to play a man's part in this catastrophic time. In any case, I really had enough problems of my own, and did not consider it my duty to act as an adviser as well as a worker, all for 4p an hour. So, after three weeks, I simply didn't go any more, and got myself another job in a vicarage, where at least, I thought, the problems would be spiritual rather than sexual.

My friend Vi had landed a super job, or so she said, working in the canteen that had been set up for the Canadians. But, as Vi proudly related, 'It's the officers' mess, not the ordinary soldiers'.'

'Don't they mind your somewhat down-to-earth language, Vi? Perhaps they think it adds a bit of colour to life.'

Certainly Vi did well, in more ways than one. Many mysterious parcels found their way into her house and supplemented the meagre rations. Less mysterious were the late night visitors. If I had had any doubts about why they stayed until the small hours, these would have been dispelled by the muffled ululations coming through the thin walls of the bedroom next to mine. I must admit, when Vi enjoyed anything, she enjoyed it whole-heartedly. Once I said to her, tactfully I hope, 'However do you look after your five kids, go out to work, and yet stay up so late at night. Don't you get worn out?'

'Got to do it, gal. It's patriotism to keep our glorious allies happy. There's those poor boys, miles away from their loved ones; nobody to comfort them or look at the snaps of their bloody kids; nobody to admire their effing ranches and their bloody dear old mums. I do all that for them for love. Well, not only love perhaps. That, and money too. Besides, they don't seem to mind that I'm not educated and posh. Can you imagine a bloody British officer hob-nobbing with the likes of me?'

No, I couldn't, judging by the English officers that came to the vicarage. Mostly public school types with high-falutin' accents, they barely acknowledged my existence except when I had to make coffee or tea for them. Only a Major Baird was always very nice. Chiefly I think because, as he was nearly bald, corpulent, and much given to unending monologues about his home in Nottingham, the city and people, and the 'little woman', people tended to give him a wide berth. One of the officers I particularly disliked was the obnoxious Major Partridge, a cousin of the vicar's. He wasn't unlike some species of bird with his hooked nose and hooded eyes. When he had to speak, and that was as seldom as possible, he spoke to me as though I was one of the lowest and most incompetent of his rankers. The last straw came when one day he sent his jeep-driver into the kitchen to tell me that '*Major* Partridge wants some sandwiches as quickly as possible.' I marched furiously into the lounge, where he was holding forth to the vicar and a few other officers, and interrupted him: '*Mr* Partridge, if you require food in this house, ask for it yourself in the proper manner, with a please and thank you. Don't send one of your minions as though I was in the army and under your command. I'm not, thank heaven, and I don't and never will take orders from you.' Deathly silence descended on them and I marched out in triumph. George, his jeep-driver, was convulsed with stifled laughter. 'Bloody marvellous, Mrs Powell. What a turn up for the book. Can't wait to get back to the depot to tell the lads, and see their faces beam. What a telling-off for the bloody "keep-em-at-it". Blimey, gal, he'll have it in for us, but it was worth it to see his face. I could have laughed fit to burst.'

Major Partridge's nick-name was 'old keep-em-at-it', from his habit of always saying to the sergeant when the men were on parade, 'Keep them at it, sergeant, keep them at it.'

The vicar, Mr Goodson, was considerably annoyed at my temerity, but his wife just laughed, saying, 'I'm sure he will keep out of Margaret's hair in future. We need her more than we do him.'

Chapter 10

Albert wrote to say that he was leaving Bridlington for Uxbridge, where he would be taking the M.P.s course.

'I shan't be sorry to leave here, Margaret, it's nothing but parades. Even on Sunday we have a church parade. I think it's daft, parading men to church. Not one in fifty ever went to church in civvy life, and they want even less to go now, on their one day of rest. Dive-Bomber Jones is a scream. When we had the first church parade, he asked for leave to fall out.

' "What for?" asked the corporal.

' "Well it's like this, corp. When me old Mum got twins, after eight singles, she was bloody mad. So when the bloody blood-and-thunder Rev told her 'it was the will of God', Ma told him she'd thank the bloody Gawd not to interfere in her family life. He'd got his bloody work cut out to save our souls, without nosing into my old man's 'bit'. You should have seen that Rev's face, we laughed fit to burst. Ma told me to keep away from the Almighty after that." Even our corporal laughed, Margaret, but Dive-Bomber wasn't allowed to fall out.'

Albert had already decided to fail the police course. He'd realised that they were very unpopular men. Men are peculiar creatures. When I wrote to tell Albert that perhaps he wouldn't have to try to fail the course, he might very well fail for natural reasons, he was very indignant and told me he could do it 'off his head' —whatever that meant.

Nevertheless, he did fail the course. 'Thank heaven,' he wrote, 'Uxbridge and the police course is the home and source of bullshit. It's nothing but inspections, beds, boots, uniforms, guns. The new intake even had an inspection for "clap"; though how we were supposed to have caught that when we were all deadbeat with drill and marches I don't know. As Dive-Bomber said,

"Only those of us with bloody flat stomachs know our vital functions are bloody well still there." I shall get some leave at the end of this course and we'll have a celebration.'

This news created no great expectations in me. By the sound of it the only kind of celebration that interested me would definitely not be on. We hadn't enough money to have a wild Walpurgis night, but I was determined to give Albert some kind of aphrodisiac. After all, it might have to last me a long time. I consulted my friend Vi, as a great deal of her conversation was devoted to the vagaries and exploits of her husband's 'thing'. Sometimes I felt I knew more about her Alf's object, than I did about Albert's.

'Blimey, gal, I've never had to worry. My f—— trouble is how to keep that bloody Alf's down. What about sunflower seeds, don't those Chinamen chew them or something. Gawd knows they have enough kids so they must be always at it.'

The possibility of acquiring sunflower seeds, and the even remoter possibility of getting Albert to masticate them before retiring upstairs was too unlikely to even contemplate. I just had to rely on my own amatory powers.

When Albert came home after three months' absence, I was more than slightly taken aback to see how fit and well he looked. After reading some of his lurid descriptions of unimaginable hardships, I expected to find a wan and drooping man, a mere shadow of his former self. Instead, Albert looked as though he'd just spent a month at a health farm. I'm afraid that I rather acidly commented that their food rations must be considerably more nourishing than ours.

'It's not that, dear. Now that I have failed the course, and while I'm waiting for a posting, I'm what is known as "attached police". So I get the good life without any of the resentment and antipathy. The M.P.s, stores and cookhouse form a clan, and I'm well in with all three. I'm allowed to make tea and sandwiches, ad lib. And as I'm "attached police", I only do occasional guard duty. Most of the time I'm in the cookhouse; I've got a mate there. But the course was an absolute nightmare; all bull-shit. Kit inspection, where all our gear had to be laid out on the bed in symmetrical order. A hairbrush pointing one inch in the wrong direction and you were on jankers. Most of the evenings were spent polishing our boots till they shone like patent leather, blancoing our webbing and brassoing our buttons. We had to stand so rigidly at attention on inspection that some of the men even slept that way. It sure wasn't a piece of cake, I can tell you.'

Our sons, who had expected to hear tales of heroic deeds, such as rescuing airmen from burning planes, or waving off or down the dawn patrol, were somewhat sceptical about their father's rôle in the Great War. The eldest, Harry, asked his Dad, 'When are you going to be a real airman, Dad? I want to tell the kids at school about the aeroplane that you keep flying.'

Up to now Albert hadn't been anywhere near any planes, grounded, burning or airborne; neither, if he had anything to do with it, would he, and I felt that our Harry would have little chance of relating tales of his heroic Dad. Good job too; I'd sooner have a live husband than a dead hero. Our grateful country's appreciation of dead heroes is not such as to enable their loved ones to live a life free from financial worries.

I can't say that, as regards our love life, Albert's leave was an unqualified success. *He* appeared happy and satisfied, but I found it rather disconcerting, and not at all conducive to transports of passion, to hear at crucial moments, 'I wonder what my mates are doing now?' or, 'I bet old Jock is just having a last visit to the cookhouse. Nothing old Jock likes more than a cup of tea at night.'

More in exasperation than righteous wrath, I hissed, 'Well, they can't be doing the same as us, or if they are, they're doing it the wrong way. And it certainly seems as though old Jock isn't the only one who seems to require just a cup of tea at night. For heaven's sake, get your mind off the camp and on to your immediate responsibilities.'

Still, one can't have it all ways—in conjunction with the previous paragraph that statement sounds a bit ambiguous. What I meant was, that Albert was a marvellous person when it came to getting our home straight. In this terrace house that my Mother had found for me, three up and three down with a huge attic, our furniture was lost. Albert put up shelves; painted the staircase; white-washed the kitchen and the outside—and only—

lavatory; executed some dozens of spiders who, by the size of their webs, had decided to inhabit our loo for life; exterminated innumerable slugs in the bit of garden, and varnished the bedroom floors in the absence of money to buy other covering. In fact, by the time Albert's leave was up, I was more than satisfied with the transformation of our home. Even Vi envied me for having Albert when she saw how hard he had worked.

'My Alf wouldn't do a hand's turn in the home, Margaret. When he gets back from the docks, all he does is flop in a chair, eat the grub and down to the boozer. Bloody hell, I tell him, can't you stir up and do a bit in the home?'

But as I pointed out to Vi, her Alf's sphere of activity in the home was confined to one particular region. As I say, you can't have it all ways.

Vi was really good for my ego because she loved to hear me use all the long words, words that she had never heard of. She used to talk to the Canadian officers at the canteen where she worked about her clever next-door neighbour; once she brought one in to see me, a Major Cameron, an exceedingly handsome and intelligent man. I knew enough about a lot of subjects, painting, archaeology, anthropology and other such matters, to be able to maintain an erudite conversation—so long as it didn't go on too long. It really was a great pleasure to be able to converse with Major Cameron. I skilfully directed the conversation to his country, and in particular his province, Alberta, saying it must be a great place, what with such marvellous arable land, the thousands of cattle, the prairie in the centre, and the high peaks of the Rocky Mountains. Major Cameron was astonished and delighted that I knew all this about his province. Naturally, I didn't mention that I had recently joined an evening class on geography and we were studying the provinces of Canada. 'Wait till I write to my wife and tell her about this, she'll never believe it. She always says that what England knows about us Canadians could be written on the back of a stamp.' Out came the photographs of Mrs Cameron and kids, and his aged parents who lived in Edmonton, having emigrated there from Glasgow years ago. I was so engrossed with this lovely man that I, and Major Cameron too, completely forgot Vi sitting there. I should have had more sense, for, although Vi had brought him to show me off, she hadn't reckoned on being a complete nonentity. Well, I lost out in the long run, for Vi never brought him or anybody else again. When I made enquiries she said, vaguely, that the officers were all too busy for any social life.

The day after Albert returned to Uxbridge we had an air-raid. It killed an elderly couple who had come to live in Hove to escape the bombs in London. A bomb fell on the gas-holder and flames shot up. As the children's school was in the vicinity we all rushed madly down there, afraid for our families. Vi was screaming imprecations on every German, but all was well. The following morning there were police and an ambulance along our street. A woman a few doors along had tried to commit suicide. She was a very quiet and unassuming person about forty, with some half-dozen kids. Her reason for trying to gas herself was that she had received a letter from her husband in the forces saying that he wouldn't be coming home. He and one of the WAAFs had fallen in love. Poor Mrs Parker, she was just as much a war casualty as anybody who had received a physical wound. We shared her family around until her parents came down from Burnley. I went to see her in the hospital. She was still in a state of shock; she simply couldn't believe that such things could happen to her.

'We had been married eighteen years,' she said, 'and in all that time my Fred never once went off the rails. He's always been a very loving husband and father. Whatever will the children do now? What kind of a woman must she be to break up a happy home?'

How could I explain to Mrs Parker that her absence and the WAAF's propinquity were the root cause. That so many marriages had lasted so long, merely because the opportunity had been lacking to change the habit of marriage.

Albert was still 'attached police', and wrote to say that there had been high-jinks the day before. Most of the ordinary soldiers had been allowed to have a night out in town and had gone there in the liberty bus. When by eleven o'clock very few had returned, the M.P.s, including Albert, went out to look for them. 'We scooped them up from everywhere. Mostly they were blind drunk on the pavement and in the gutters. In the pubs, it looked as though a free-for-all had been going on all evening. In one pub, the landlady, a formidable fifteen stoner, was laying about the soldiers with a broom. When we finally got them back to camp, one joker rang the fire alarm, and the whole camp had to turn out. There was the choleric major saying "Where's the fire, where is it?" and everybody standing around in the freezing cold in various stages of undress. As we weren't the culprits we had much ado to suppress our laughter. In fact, we didn't suppress it when the ambulance drove up to carry away the "fire victims". When they opened the ambulance doors they discovered that it was full of firewood, hoarded there by somebody in preparation for cold nights. I'll be leaving here in a day or two, I'll let you know where to. Pity I have to be graded, I'm enjoying myself here, I can tell you.'

He needn't have bothered to tell me. I could sense it by his letters and his leave.

Chapter 11

My job at the vicarage having finished through circumstances beyond my control, I started another, working for the widow of a bank manager. She lived in a luxury flat along with two cats, a dog and two budgerigars to console her for the recent loss of a husband. According to the porter of the block of flats, Mrs Bellamy also consoled herself in other ways, judging by the empty bottles in her dustbin. I subsequently discovered he was right about that. Little do all the tenants of these flats realise that nothing about their lives is hidden from the porters.

I liked Mrs Bellamy, she treated me as a person. None of that making tea or coffee and leaving me to drink mine in the kitchen while she sat in the lounge.

'You know, Mrs Powell,' she'd start off in a somewhat lachry-mose manner, 'Mr Bellamy was the absolute soul of uprightness and probity. Never in all his life did he drink alcohol or smoke. In bed by ten o'clock every night. Every year we spent two weeks' holiday at the same place in the country. His whole life was the bank, and he was always telling me how much his service was appreciated.'

Here Mrs Bellamy's narrative would alter in tone, assisted, I suspect by the liberal doses of whisky in her tea. 'It was as well for him that he was appreciated at the bank, for he certainly wasn't anywhere else. A bigger, pompous bore I have yet to meet. He never had a thought that he hadn't first dissected, put through a sieve and then dried out in case there was any life left in it. Why, I get more fun out of these animals here than ever I got out of Mr Bellamy. I could have repeated, word for word, all his conversation, both before he went off to the bank, and after dinner in the evening. Then it was a peck on the cheek, and into bed. Once, in desperation, I put my arms round him and kissed him on the mouth. Honestly, Mrs Powell, by the expression on his face, you'd have thought I was the original "scarlet woman".

By now, abandoning all pretence, Mrs Bellamy would start on the whisky, incidentally pouring out a liberal libation for me, and a few drops for Mimi, the poodle, to show she loved her more than Peter and Paul, the cats.

'Mr Bellamy "passed over" six months ago,' and here she began to giggle, 'I suppose you could say he "passed out" too, at the age of sixty-four, leaving a sorrowing widow. I woke up one morning and there he was beside me with life extinct. Well, Margaret,' (I was Margaret by now) 'these last twenty years, for all you could tell in bed, life always was extinct. I think that he kept "it" locked up in the vaults in the bank. His job needed all the vital forces. The doctor said that Mr Bellamy died of heart failure. He was quite shocked when I said it wasn't through over-working at home.'

As she poured out yet more whisky I thought what a lovely job this was, just sit there and nod sympathetically at intervals; Mrs Bellamy nursing Mimi and I with Peter and Paul on my lap.

'Mr Bellamy's twin brother came to see us about ten years ago. Just returned from Australia to settle down in England. Apart from the likeness, Margaret, you would never have thought they were brothers, let alone twins. Paul's nature was as different from my Peter's as chalk from cheese—that's why I call my cats, Peter and Paul. My brother-in-law was an extrovert, casual in dress, very outspoken and as lively as a cricket. He dumbfounded and embarrassed Peter by the tales of his sexual exploits in Australia; I was fascinated. Oh, Margaret, I got the wrong man, if only I'd met Paul first. The only surprise I ever got from Mr Bellamy was to discover the amount of money he left, at least three times as much as I expected. I knew we lived a quiet life, but I never thought he had saved so much. That's him hanging on the wall there. Doesn't he look the epitome of dullness and respectability? His eyes follow you around the room, a perpetual reminder of the narrow path to heaven. Still, he left me well off. Let's have another drink and raise our glasses to that model husband.'

By now, with the amount we had consumed, we could hardly

see the wall, let alone his portrait. But we raised our glasses in the general direction in reverent silence.

'You know what, Margaret, I'm going to splash out on new clothes and be a real "Merry Widow"; who knows what might come along?'

Unfortunately, Mrs Bellamy had none of the desirable attributes of a Merry Widow. It would have required more imagination than I had to visualise Lehar writing an operetta for Maisie Bellamy. Faded, fat and fiftyish, I just couldn't imagine her changing, or what incentive she would find. I was wrong, for the incentive came to her door in the person of Paul, her brother-in-law. I hadn't known him long before I could tell that the magnet which drew him was his sister-in-law's money. He certainly was a charmer; I could easily have fallen for him myself. Looking at least ten years younger than his sixty-four years, with his slim figure and a mass of wavy grey hair, he kept us entranced with his tales of life in Australia, the hardships of starting out there, the miles of barren land, the aborigines. Never could he have had a more fascinated and appreciative audience than us. Maisie blossomed in his presence like a rose sprinkled with dew; she became a new woman. I had a natural advantage in that I was twenty years younger, but then I was neither wealthy nor a widow. Paul's attentions to me were strictly confined to the periods when Maisie was out. He merely laughed when I said, 'You haven't really fallen in love with Maisie. If your brother had left her without a penny, we would never have seen you here—or not for long.'

'Well, so what? You've seen in this last month the difference in Maisie, how young and happy she looks. Why, she's even become quite witty in a conversational way. What's the harm in my helping her to spend her money and have a bit of fun. It's better for her than the whisky bottle. And a decent home and a warm bed mean more to me than sharing a bed-sitter with a succession of sculpin' sheilas. Maisie and me will get on well together, you'll see. In the meantime, there's you and me here, so why waste time?'

'Why, indeed,' I answered, eluding his amatory embraces. 'Maisie pays me to keep the flat clean, so I won't waste time.

Especially as Albert will be home on leave tomorrow.'

Albert's last letter, after a rather brief enquiry as to my own and the children's welfare, and an even more perfunctory enquiry about my Mother, went on to say that he had been sent to Escrick village, to work on a bomb dump.

'Will Dad drop the bombs on the Germans?' the children asked me, after I read that bit of the letter to them. 'Will he fire them in cannons over the water to them Germans?' asked my youngest.

'No, he will not be dropping the bombs on anybody, unless he drops one on his toe. And you don't put bombs in a cannon; you are thinking of shells.'

The boys promptly lost interest in their Father as a potential contestant in this war. In fact, I was afraid that they were beginning to forget him altogether—as indeed was happening in so many families. The wives, including me, were assuming the rôle of the father, and liking it. Especially where the man had always been the boss, this new-found freedom was heady wine to the husbandless wife. For the first time in their married life perhaps, the wives were making the decisions, handling all the money, dealing with tradesmen, rent collectors and other matters of finance. For the first time, there was nobody to say, 'Where are you going? Who with? What time will you be in?' In comparative freedom the wives could have neighbours in for a gossip, mind each other's kids while they had a night out at a film, joke and laugh in the local with soldiers without a glowering husband ready to burst with rage. Yes, indeed, the women were being liberated all right.

'Up here in Escrick, Yorkshire, it's like another world; if it wasn't for the uniformed men, you'd never know there was a war on, it's so quiet and peaceful. A dozen of us arrived at the same time, and the village policeman took us round to various private billets. When it got to my turn, he said, "You're lucky, it's a farm for you," and he was right. I tell you, Margaret, it's as good as living at home, they treat me so well. Meals with the family, sit in their lounge afterwards talking and reading. And the food—it's out of this world. Plates piled high with meat, fresh veg., lovely butter and bacon and eggs galore.'

I read all this out to the children as we sat at lunch consuming half of our weekly meat ration in one fell swoop—at 1/2d worth each per week, the meat was by no means piled on our plates. 'Isn't it nice to know that your Father, without the pleasure and comfort of us around him, isn't suffering any hardship! Far from us sending him a food parcel, boys, perhaps we can expect him to send one to us. What delicacy shall we ask him for? What about a dozen eggs?'

Our egg ration didn't work out at one each a week, and although Lord Woolton went to great lengths to assure us that the dried egg allowance was just as nutritional—perhaps it was —it certainly didn't taste like new-laid ones. As for the bread, although it wasn't rationed, fortunately, as my three sons seemed to eat like horses, we housewives didn't thank Lord Woolton when he introduced the National Loaf. Made of wholemeal flour, it was dark, coarse and, we considered, indigestible. But we were all so hungry, we ate it. That bread, and potatoes—also un-rationed—were our staple diet.

'What does Dad do with the bombs if he isn't going to drop them on the Germans?' asked David. 'What is Dad doing? Does he tell you in the letter, Mum?'

'Well, here's what Dad writes: "Every day, outside the village pub called the Hare and Hounds, we have roll-call, to make sure that we are all there. Then we march to the middle of the woods nearby where there is a bomb dump and wait for a lorry load of bombs to arrive. Our job is to unload them, stack them in a heap, then camouflage the pile with branches from the trees. We have our matches and cigarettes taken away before we start, but gen-erally one of us manages to hide some so that as soon as the officer has gone we have a quiet smoke. It's the life of Riley here, I'm already putting on weight." '

'Would a bomb explode if Dad dropped it?' my youngest son, Phillip, asked, only to be squashed by Harry, who informed him that bombs have to be dropped from a plane before they go off. As I was by no means sure of this myself, I let them argue it out. Their Father was receiving more attention from them in his absence than ever he did when at home.

I was sorry to hear from Mrs Bellamy that she was leaving

Hove to go and live with her brother-in-law Paul. Though I wasn't surprised, as Paul had been working towards this all through the last month. Maisie was quite carried away with the excitement of her new life. As we sat, knocking back copious glasses of gin, she bubbled over.

'I'm going to have a marvellous time with Paul, Margaret, he's so different from Peter. They look alike, but that's all. Paul is so warm and alive, not dried up and desiccated like his brother was. You know, this will be the first time in all my life that I haven't been virtuous. Gin and sin, who'd have thought it was so exciting, and at my time of life too?'

Well, it was exciting in those days to deviate from the path of virtue. Women who did so felt that they were striking a blow for freedom, for liberation from the claustrophobic life of home and family; that they too, as men had done for years, albeit perhaps more discreetly, could live a life unshackled by the chains of the church and public opinion. The innovation of birth control clinics created a far greater impact, both socially and morally, than did the revolution of the Pill at a far later date.

Birth control was, in the eyes of the Church and strict moralists of a Victorian age, a threat not only to chastity but to the institution of marriage itself. It was an open invitation to sin with impunity. A lot of women did. And they sinned with gay abandon, with joy in their sexual freedom. Affairs were nothing like the sad and apathetic doings of today. Nowadays, when people change partners as often as they do at a Paul Jones dance, the thrill and daring are no more.

Maisie gave me ten pounds before she moved. Paul, who had no money, offered to let me take it out in trade. What a colossal nerve that man had. He may have been very well-endowed, but he was nearly thirty years older than me.

When I told my friend Vi Davis, she just laughed and said, 'Any port in a storm, love.' It was just as well for Vi that Alf, her husband, came down to see her whenever he could get away from the docks. Much to Vi's fury and dismay, she was pregnant again after five years, and wondering whether or not it was Alf who had got her that way. Although when she dressed up Vi wasn't a bad looking woman, before the war, living near the docks in London, the opportunities for dalliance with men had been practically non-existent. Small wonder that Vi had really gone to town with all the spare men around at the canteen. She said that it wasn't her fault. It was living in Hove, inhaling all that ozone, that put new life into her. It surely had now, literally speaking.

At the beginning of the war Vi had joined the official evacuation with her five youngest children. I never tired of listening to her hilarious account of this event.

'I went with my friend, Dot Harris. She had two toddlers and a baby of six weeks. There must have been thousands of us at the railway station, and a bloody sight we must have looked. The kids were lumbered up with gas masks, packets of sandwiches, and a few bits and pieces in a parcel or pillow case. They stuck us in a train with no corridor, my five kids, and Dot with her three. Talk about a bloody shambles. In no time at all the kids were whining for a lavatory, and in the end they wet all over the seats. Their faces were smothered in chocolate and we had no water to clean them up. When we got to the other end we were miles from anywhere.

' "My gawd," screeched Dot, "bloody no-man's-land! Where's the shops and people? Nothing but a bloody cow and a lot of grass."

'Some mothers took one look and crossed straight over to the other side of the station to get a train back. The one and only station worker said there wouldn't be a train until the morning, but they refused to budge in case they missed it. All the kids without mothers got taken off in buses. At the end there were about a dozen families left and people who had offered to take in evacuees came and looked us over as though we were cattle in the market. They wanted to split my kids up, but I said not bloody likely you don't, we ain't come all this way to be parted. At last the snooty old dame that owned the big house said we could live in the servants' quarters as they were all away doing war-work—and I bet they never came back to her. The only servant she had left was an ancient old crow who'd been with the family for years. I should think the house had been built in the year dot; it was as cold as charity. There were three servants' bedrooms, so Dot and me had one each with the youngest kids, and the others mucked in together. There was a bathroom with a lot of silly china birds on one wall. My Lily promptly broke one, and the youngest kids screamed blue murder at getting in the bath—they'd never seen one before. You should have seen that old crone's face when the kids hopped into bed in their shirts. She'd never known kids who didn't have pyjamas and nightdresses. Blimey, what a dump it was. One village shop, the nearest fish and chip shop was five miles away and the buses only ran twice a week. When Dot and me went into the local it was like a bloody funeral parlour. You could have heard a pin drop when she asked for her usual "half up the spout"—that was half a pint of stout.

'What with that, and that old family retainer everlastingly nagging at the kids, we decided to go back to London. That old dragon told Dot she didn't know when she was well off. Old Dot gave her a mouthful. "We'd sooner face bloody Hitler and his bombs than have to look at your phizog every morning." When we got back to the docks we found that half the street had come back. Fed up with all that fresh air and only bloody cows for company.'

Albert's next letter was a long tale of woe. The so-an-so corporal had got Albert removed from his cushy billet and installed himself there.

'He's a puffed-up pompous jackass who thinks that being a corporal is almost equivalent to air-commodore. His excuse for taking my billet is that he has an ulcer and needs special food. He should be in sick-bay if that's true. These nice people, the Roberts, refused to take him at first, saying they saw no reason why they should change their airman—I had already done a lot of "stirring-up" in anticipation. But the corporal went to the C.O. who had me on the carpet, accusing me of creating discord.

' "You know there is a war on, 1472968, and whether or not your billet meets with your approval is of no importance whatsoever."

'Mrs Roberts was so annoyed at losing me that she wouldn't let the corporal sit with them for meals, he had to eat in the kitchen and then sit in his bedroom. So he complained again to the C.O. Next thing I know is, the C.O. says get in the car. He drives me to Snaith, drops me at the main gate and tells me, "This is the end of the line for you, from here on you are on your own." This is what's known as posting on attachment, or in other words, getting rid of a troublesome airman.'

When I read this story of world-shaking incidents in Albert's life, I felt really heartened to know that amidst all the appalling filth and horror of the war, the petty little details of life were still going on. On went the saga of his great day.

'When I went before the S.W.O. he says, "Ah! 1472968, you are for the stores." For one awful moment I thought he said, "stones". I had a lightning vision of myself, stripped to the waist, exposing the hairs on my chest—all two of them—and bashing away at great rocks like the men in that film, *I was a fugitive from a chain gang.*'

In my wildest moments I couldn't imagine Albert being a fugitive from anything, let alone a chain gang.

'You know, Margaret, working in the stores is a good number. Once again, I've landed on my feet—I must be good at happy landings. The sergeant took to me straight away, for he said, "Thank heaven they have sent me a good chap. The last one they sent made me a nervous wreck. Every time I went by he sprang to attention and saluted. When I told him I wasn't the C.O. and didn't want all that bloody bull-shit, he looked as though I'd wounded him to death."'

Well, well. That sergeant must be very perceptive to know that Albert is a good chap in five minutes. Albert sure is lucky. Unlike the prophet who is without honour in his own country, Albert seems to be with honour wherever he goes. I search through the letter for a loving word and enquiries about how I am surviving the ordeal of his absence and the anxiety of looking after the three boys. I search in vain. There's just a line at the end of the letter to say he will be home on leave soon.

Actually, I was perfectly happy at being the only parent. I liked making all the decisions and not having to consult Albert. I couldn't do all the jobs that Albert was so good at, such as decorating the home and mending the boys' shoes—although my Mother could do all that for us in the last war. But now *I* had a milkman who was always ready to mend a fuse or put on a tap washer; he even killed a mouse in my larder. He was much too old for any form of dalliance, but one can't have everything, especially in war time.

It was difficult to generate a feeling of excitement in my sons when I told them that their father was working in the stores—it was so reminiscent of the grocer's. In any case Harry was immersed in exams to the exclusion of outside interests. It was also difficult, when I knew that Albert was so well-fed, to go easy on our rations so that I could, metaphorically speaking, kill the fatted calf for him. I decided to make him one of those superb sugarless cakes, using lard, vinegar and one dried egg, from the recipe in one of the Government leaflets. I'd already got Meals without Meat. Unfortunately, as fruit was practically non-existent, and Albert disliked ginger, or caraway seeds, the making of a cake did present some problems. A friend of mine had tried adding mashed carrots; the resultant mess was uneatable unless one was absolutely starving. We were constantly being exhorted by the Government and Lord Woolton to eat more carrots; for suddenly, after years of being just a humble vegetable, fit only for stews or garnish, carrots were discovered to be pearls beyond price, rich in vitamins, 'jewels from the good earth'. They even helped you to see in the dark. Nevertheless the stubborn housewives still preferred dried fruit in their cakes and puddings rather than grated carrot.

I must say that Albert, always smart in appearance, looked quite someone in his Air Force uniform. By now he had put on some weight and it really fitted him. Fortunately, our sons were resigned to the fact that they would hear no thrilling accounts of heroic deeds and hair-breadth escapes. Apart from the uniform he was just the same Dad as before the war. He was just the same husband too; the glamour stopped short at the uniform. When we came back from the pub on his first evening home, the conversation was a continuation of his letters.

'This posting to Snaith is the start of another happy chapter in my service life. The officers are splendid, especially the Squadron and Pilot. Working at the stores I'm excused all parades and duties. Life is a piece of cake. As for the Warrant Officer, he's a great comedian, a great joker. To give you an example, the other day, when the WAAFs complained that the path to their loo was dark and dangerous at night, he lined them up—all six of them—and escorted them personally. He held hands with the prettiest, Doris—or Dorise as she likes it pronounced.'

Well apart from the fact that I neither expected, nor wanted, Albert's first night of leave—and love I hoped—to be devoted to yet more anecdotes of his service life, for the life of me I couldn't see how this story established the W.O. as a wit. It seemed to me that humour in the Forces must be down to the lowest common denominator. However, like a dutiful wife, I laughed, while inwardly hoping to persuade Albert to forget for a while his other existence.

In my efforts to take his mind off distant delights and prove that I too could be as amusing as the W.O., I told him about Vi being pregnant and the apprehensions she had about whether the new arrival would look like her Alf, or be a composite of all the various elements of our 'glorious allies' who had received comfort from Vi. I'm sure that I made an hilarious story out of this material, but Albert didn't even smile, which infuriated me, as in one of his letters there had been a long account of the sexual exploits of a certain L.A.C. in the camp. This Lothario had, according to Albert, the ability to knock over the girls like nine-pins with his physical charms. He was constantly to be found either in an upright or horizontal position with some female, in or out of uniform, who appeared to be so overcome with ecstasy that she was practically in a trance. All this in spite of the fact that this Lothario was married and had a family. But in Albert's book, as in most men's, it was all right for the man if he could get away with it. Being promiscuous was an inherent part of the nature of a man; he wasn't expected to be virtuous, that was a woman's duty.

Give Vi her due, although in the milieu of London's East End she could have found a back street abortionist, she never seriously considered it. 'For Gawd's sake, let the little b—— at least see what the bloody world's like outside. Besides, while I've got to wait six months for him, I don't need to worry about my night life.' It was a matter of astonishment to me that Vi, who worked hard at the canteen and had five kids to look after, always seemed to have abundant energy at night. In our local pub, which incidentally had to be avoided like the plague when Albert was home, old Vi was as good as a cabaret turn to the proprietors.

And, as Vi discovered, being pregnant in war time had other advantages than sexual freedom; a mother-to-be immediately became a special object in the eyes of Lord Woolton, who appeared to be determined that the next generation should at least arrive strong and healthy. To Vi's delight, she became entitled to extra cheese, eggs and meat, and a free pint of milk every day. But best of all, she got a green ration book, which definitely was one-upmanship, for it entitled the holder to go to the head of any queue waiting for their rations. It was a sight to bring tears to the stoutest heart to see Vi, like a ship in full sail, with a flotilla of kids in her wake, triumphantly holding her green book aloft, and majestically making her way to the front of a queue of ordinary housewives who had been standing for nearly an hour.

My Mother never really liked Vi, but not because of her amoral life. Mother was philosophical over that, saying that opportunity and propinquity were obviously tempting. What Mother could never understand was why Vi could never get serious about the war, whereas, to Mother, the war was foul and iniquitous, and the men, whose blunders and lack of statesmanship had allowed it to happen, even more so. Especially did Mother include Chamberlain in her indictment. She considered that it was his policy of appeasement that had led to this World War II, and that a man who could state, as Chamberlain did in September 1938; 'How horrible, fantastic, incredible it is, that we should be digging trenches and trying on gas-masks here, because of a quarrel between people of whom we know nothing', was suffering from the worse form of self-delusion. For they were not people of whom we knew nothing. We might not have known a great deal about the Czechoslovaks, but we certainly knew from past experience what the Germans were like.

Mother's attitude to this war had changed after the tragedy of our shattered Expeditionary Force. About a quarter of a million soldiers had to be rescued from Dunkirk, and among them was her youngest son, Donald, my best-beloved brother. The weary and terrible hours went by, as all those hundreds of little craft, manned by heroic amateurs, brought back the Dunkirk survivors, and still we heard nothing of Donald. Then came the card, 'alive and well'; it was a blessed miracle.

'Thank heaven for Churchill,' said my Mother. 'Now that he is in command, we shall win this war, and it will be a war to end all wars. He will see to it that Germany never has the chance to re-arm again, as they did after the last war. We are fighting for a purpose, for freedom and democracy.'

Mother was really indignant when I remarked, 'Don't you think, Mum, that the words freedom and democracy are somewhat ironical when applied to us, a country which has colonised a considerable portion of the world? Do you think that the inhabitants of our colonies feel "free and democratic"? Still, don't worry, Mum. When this war is over we shall probably find we have nothing left but our Commonwealth. Even if we win the war, we shall have won nothing concrete. Gone are the days when the victors acquired land, loot and universal acclaim. Now all are execrated, winners and losers. We shall probably find, after this war, that the peoples to whom we brought the inestimable benefits of our civilisation, are singularly lacking in gratitude. So much so, in fact, that, astonishing as it may seem, they prefer to govern themselves.'

My Father very seldom joined in these arguments over the conduct and results of the war. He was horrified at the appalling deaths of civilians and destruction of property through air-raids. He could not understand how a government could say that the enemy raids stiffened the morale of the British, while our raids on Germany were having the opposite effect, as though that nation was morally inferior to us. After July 1943, the week of the ghastly and horrific British incendiary air-raid on Hamburg, in which the conflagration caused total destruction and the heat killed people even in the bomb proof shelters, my Father lost all faith in England as a civilised country.

'When you think, Nell, that only two weeks after the declaration of war, Neville Chamberlain stated, "Whatever the lengths to which others may go, His Majesty's Government will never resort to deliberate attack on women and children just for the sake of terrorism", and now this bestial and obscene killing of them all in Hamburg. Every foul and evil deed leaves a residue of corruption which permeates the very air we breathe. Even in war there must surely be a limit beyond which man's conscience will not let him go; some atrocity from which he recoils in shame.'

But this war involved all, civilians and combatants alike. The churches, whose *raison d'être* was to preach peace and goodwill to all men, were singularly at a loss. It was hardly in accordance with their professed faith to tell the congregation, 'We British are right to rain death and destruction on innocent women and children because our cause is right.'

Chapter 12

Albert was still enjoying a peaceful existence, far away from the alarums and upheavals of civilian life. His main complaint was the discomfort of the Nissen hut in which he slept. 'There are about twenty men in our hut, all of different ages, behaviour, learning and certainly different notions of hygiene. Our hut, Margaret, is teeming with life. Mice, spiders and earwigs are here in abundance. I can stick that. It's the men that flit in and out like a dog at a fair. They change so often that I'm never sure who will be in the next bed. Sometimes I feel we are playing musical chairs, and somebody will be left standing. But for a welcome change, I have had the same man next to me for at least two weeks. He's a Tynesider, Shorty, and as tough as old boots. When he's been into town he comes back as drunk as a lord and starts to sing bawdy songs in a really melodious voice. Unfortunately, he hasn't even an elemental idea of cleanliness, and the reek from his bed is enough to form a poisonous gas over mine, however much I stick my nose under the blankets. You would have laughed at the shemozzle the other night when a fellow called Lardy—because he has a dead white face—tried to get into Shorty's bed, while he was in it. Lardy was so drunk as not to know what he was doing, but Shorty thought his virtue was in danger from the wrong sex. He leapt out of bed like a gazelle, and the language he poured out would have shrivelled the devil himself. How are you, my love? Have you started another job yet? Don't work too hard, and get old before your time.'

He should well say that. I had just given up a job where the woman must have thought she was employing a galley-slave. From the moment I arrived at nine o'clock, until I left at one o'clock, I never stopped working. Even a cup of tea had to be drunk in gulps, between jobs. About ten minutes before it was time to leave she would give me a task that took at least half an hour to do. Three weeks of her and I'd had enough.

I was now working for a really sweet old man, a Mr Borman. He told me that he suffered from hamathritis, caused by drinking too much port when he was young. I hadn't a clue what sort of complaint hamathritis was. On consulting my dictionary when I got home, I found that it meant Mr Borman had gout in all his joints. Nevertheless, he was still drinking port, and when I suggested that maybe his gout would improve if he changed to another kind of alcohol Mr Borman just laughed—I must say he seemed to enjoy his sufferings at times.

'I can't give it up at my time of life, Mrs Powell; it's become an addiction. To refrain from port would be worse than the tortures of my gout. It's really your sex that started me on this passion. My Mother died when I was six and left me in the care of my five, much older, sisters. John Knox's "Monstrous Regiment of Women" couldn't have been more interfering and dictatorial than were my sisters. Everything that I said, and did, was subject to their mostly disapproving scrutiny. But the event that annoyed them most happened on my sixteenth birthday for, after dinner that night, when we all rose from the table leaving my Father to drink his port, my Father called me back. He said that now I was old enough to drink a glass of port and smoke a cigar after dinner each night. The horrified expression on the faces of my sisters—all spinsters and likely to remain so—gladdened my heart. They remonstrated with our Father, saying I was far too young, that my health would be permanently impaired, that Mother on her deathbed and with her dying breath had entrusted them with the sacred task of looking after me. "What utter rubbish you cackling females talk," sarcastically replied Father, "your Mother never had a thought in her head for anybody but herself all her life, and if she uttered anything with her dying breath, which I very much doubt, it would only have been to consign me to perdition. Be off with you, to your knitting or crochet or whatever five finicking females do of an evening. You've had Jerome for ten years and now I'm going to do the rest." I tell you Mrs Powell, it was the finest time of all my sixteen years—though I must admit I didn't enjoy the cigar.'

Albert's war service seemed to be somewhat peripatetic, for the next letter had a different postmark. Once again he had been posted and once again he was attached police. This move was to Topcliff, where they actually had planes, Wellingtons and Lancasters.

'The Geordie, Shorty, came with me, and we are both attached police. Nobody at Topcliff had received any notification that we were on our way. The corporal assigned us to a hut, and said that we would be sent for. Such is the hugeness of this camp, we had two glorious days before officialdom knew we were there. Shorty and I had the time of our lives. We kept out of sight except when we queued up at the cook house. Finally, they realised that these were two spare airmen without an allocated task. I was put on night-guard duty at the gate. I wear a belt with a holster, and have a Colt automatic with a round of bullets. I feel a bit like a modern Wild Bill Hickok. Except that he was lightning on the draw, while I can't get the blasted pistol out of the holster. Believe me, I never put the bullets in the pistol as I haven't the remotest idea how to fire it. Why I might inadvertently touch the trigger and shoot myself. It's a mighty lonely job sitting in the sentry box when it's pitch dark outside and there isn't a soul to talk to. After a while, listening and gazing into the darkness, you imagine there's someone out there waiting to leap on to you. I got an awful shock the other night. I could just faintly see a shape which looked to be crouched down and creeping towards me. I called out "Who goes there?" in the accepted manner, but obviously the intruder had no knowledge of English, for there was no reply. Carefully taking hold of my pistol by the barrel, I got ready to bash whatever it was when, luckily for me, the shape barked. It was a very large collie dog. I'll be jolly glad when my two weeks' guard-duty is over.'

When I read this out to my sons, omitting the part about Albert not knowing how to shoot the pistol, David heaved a sigh of relief. At last his Dad was a real airman. 'Will Dad be able to bring his Colt with him when he comes on leave? Can I take it to school to show the other boys?'

I was still working three mornings a week for Mr Borman, and incidentally developing a taste for his port. It was his birthday on one of my days, and he opened a bottle of vintage port. We each drank two glasses. The taste and fragrance were out of this world, wine of the gods, ambrosia. One of his two remaining sisters came to see him. I thought that Mr Borman was old, but his sister was positively antediluvian. Her skin was so scaly that it looked laminated. Far from being 'some remnant of history, which has casually escaped the shipwreck of time', I imagined she had been shipwrecked from the beginning of her voyage through life. Certainly, time had not mellowed her disposition or taken the edge off her caustic tongue.

The look she gave me when Mr Borman told her we had been drinking the vintage port, was likely to have turned the wine rancid. 'You know Father laid down that port for all of us. You have no right to have kept the lot. Especially as it was dear Mother's money that paid for all of it. Father was a selfish and ungrateful man; he never thought anything of us girls, and you have become just like him. Furthermore, I'll outlive you; you're killing yourself with drink and there's nobody to stop you.'

Here she looked at me maliciously, no doubt thinking it a heinous crime that a daily, who must be unable to appreciate such luxuries as vintage port, should be on such familiar terms with her brother. Mind you, she was right. Mr Borman only lived for about six months after her visit. So many of the people I worked for seemed to depart life soon after they employed me. It wasn't that I had a deleterious effect; it was because they were so old when I started. Perhaps the way I rushed through the flat, full of life and energy, made them more conscious of their own infirmities. Anyway, dear old Mr Borman gave me a bottle of the best port just before he died. I meant to keep the bottle for some epoch-making event, but its proximity was too much for my will-power, and Albert and I drank it when he was home on leave. It was like drinking velvet.

As usual, Albert's conversation was full of his service life. It was astonishing to realise how the Air Force—and probably the army would have done the same—had absorbed all of his personality. He still loved us and his home, but civilian life seemed as remote from Albert as another world. Not that I minded, I was pleased that he was happy, and I was happy at running the home and bringing up our sons on my own. Especially so as our eldest was now in a grammar school. I had promptly joined the parent-teacher association and was never averse to contributing my ideas and opinions when asked—and usually without waiting to be asked.

Albert's saga continued. 'After I had done my spell of night duty, Shorty and I were sent to a grand and lovely old mansion, Scelfield House. It was where the air-crews lived, and we were to do guard duty there for two weeks. I'll never in all my life forget what we, two attached police, saw as the door was opened. There was this great hall, with a double staircase at the end sweeping up to a balcony. And ranged up this staircase were the young air-crews. Immediately they saw us two police they simultaneously burst into an extremely bawdy song which described the inadequacies of the service, physically, mentally and definitely sexually. I know that one of the lines of the song said more of the M.P.s time should be taken up with trying to discover where their sexual appliance had disappeared to, than in chasing poor A.W.O.L.s. They were ribbing us, of course, but in a friendly way. Seeing all those laughing young men, perhaps soon never more to laugh and love again, hearing their really tuneful voices, well I'm not ashamed to tell you, Margaret, it brought a lump to my throat and tears to my eyes.

'But on a more cheerful note, we have a man in our hut who's just up your street where words are concerned. He's the gentleman of our hut; before he was called-up he was the junior partner of an estate firm—or so he says. His educated voice makes him the butt of the men, though it's mostly goodnatured, especially when he comes out with some long and high-falutin' word. He can't bear the odour that emanates from Shorty; says that Shorty suffers from osmidrosis. Shorty immediately got irate, telling him, "I'm no more a bloody bastard than you are, I was born in wedlock"—though only just, he told me afterwards. Then Claud had to explain that "osmidrosis" meant "retaining his ill-smelling sweat".

'The only men really disliked in our hut are two large and

brawny Australians. They come from South Australia, a place called Boormara, or some such name. They are forever telling us that it's God's own country out there. The other night one of them started on again, "A man has to be a real man to survive the rigours and hardships of life in our country, I can tell you. You English, living in this soft little island, haven't a hope in hell of making a living out there because you don't know what work is. Why, a couple of years ago we had one of you Britishers come out to our farm, a chap about thirty years old. After a week of getting up at five o'clock, and sweating and toiling until dark, he was a nervous wreck. Bloody spineless!"

'You'll never believe what happened after that. Shorty had just told them to shut their f—— mouths up when Claud, our posh and educated man, got off his bed and quietly walked over to Merrill—the one who had just spoken. This is just what he said to him, although I've probably spelt it wrong: "You microcephalous mountain of mush. You hulking hunk of brainless baggage. My great-grandfather at the age of sixteen was sent to Botany Bay, merely for stealing a crust of bread. He lived out there until he was ninety, under conditions you creodonts could never imagine. You two Kookaburras make me sick." And then, Margaret, he punched that Merrill on the nose and knocked him right out. I can tell you, we were all so petrified with astonishment that nobody spoke a word or moved. Bongo, the other Australian, just sat there. I think that all he understood was Kookaburra, it's a laughing jackass. We all regard our Claud with respect now. But what we didn't know at the time was that he had received a letter that morning from his home, to say that his youngest brother had been shot down over Germany. Incidentally, I could have been promoted to a corporal. But what's the use? The rise in money will benefit neither of us. They will deduct more of my pay for you, but the Government will pay you less. And I don't want to be a corporal anyway and have to start giving men orders.'

Money was fast becoming a problem now that Harry was at the grammar school. The grants I received, though a help, by no means covered the cost of the uniform and all the other impedimenta that a grammar school education seemed to demand.

Football and cricket gear, running shoes and shorts, satchel and fountain pen. Yet if I got more work, my separation allowance would be reduced accordingly. My sons were very good. The two eldest were now doing a paper round and earning about five shillings each. That certainly helped with their pocket money.

Chapter 13

Now that all the Canadians had left, Hove reverted to its normally quiet and respectable existence. But although the Canadians weren't with us physically, the aftermath of their sojourn most certainly was. Married ladies were feverishly consulting the calendar hoping that the dates of their husband's past leaves would coincide correctly with the impending arrival of the latest addition to the family—the ladies whose husbands were abroad were the most unfortunate. Young, unmarried girls were trying to placate irate and outraged parents, and some parents were writing indignant letters to the Canadian authorities to the effect that Private So-and-So must be granted leave to come back to marry their daughter. But in all fairness, many young Canadians were trying to get the necessary permission and papers over from their country, and many girls were already receiving kind letters from Canadian Mums and parcels of clothing for the forthcoming event.

My friend Vi, with five children and another on the way, was not in the least downcast. Although her job in the canteen had finished, she was by no means deprived, sexually or financially. Vi knew all the tricks of the trade when it came to getting concessions from stony-hearted and suspicious officials. She was no longer a close neighbour, a fact that occasioned me little regret, I'm afraid, since her friend, Dot Harris, was now sharing a house with her. The uproar and chaos caused by the eight children were almost indescribable. I think Dot Harris's were the worst. I never saw them otherwise than snotty-nosed and jammy-faced, and the language that Dot's four-year-old boy could use was truly appalling. Nevertheless, to see Vi and Dot after an expedition to the Citizens' Advice Bureau to enquire about their 'rights', and then on to the Council offices to make sure they got those rights, was a sight to bring comfort to any timid soul who was afraid of Bumbledom. They came back laden with blankets and clothes for the children, vouchers to get boots, and promises of future help. They had already had rows with the neighbours on either side, neither of whom were any match when it came to vituperation for Dot or Vi, not to mention Vi's two elder daughters, who occasionally came down at the weekend. I was there one Saturday afternoon when Rose, one of the daughters, was having a violent altercation with a neighbour. The description of the supposed hardships suffered by her Mother, separated from the comforts of husband and home, was enough to have melted the hardest heart; I think that the neighbour's was made of concrete. Rose was never at a loss for words; as Vi said, 'Our Rosie's been edicated.' She lambasted the woman with, 'It's people like you that make life unbearable for poor evacuees. How would you like to be stuck in this snooty town, where you didn't have any friends? How would you like to fear every day that your husband might be killed in the docks, your daughters bombed in the factory, and your sons shot to pieces by the bloody Germans? Old cows like you, with a husband too old to fight, never had any bloody kids, probably too refined to have a bit in bloody bed, or else you petrified it for him. You are just a parasite, getting kept and giving nothing. Well, you'll have to wait till this bloody war's over before you can get a "nice" neighbour. Don't worry, you won't see my Ma for dust once it's safe to take the kids back.'

Albert wasn't sorry that Vi was a few streets away. She did get on his nerves with her tendency to knock on our door at any time.

Once again Albert had been posted—this time on to Cheadle, Cheshire. I could not understand why the Air Force was giving Albert this kind of Cook's tour around England. Was it that his services were so valuable that each depot felt it would be selfish if they kept him for too long? Or were the consequences of having Albert so disastrous that he had to be moved on before total disintegration occurred? Albert didn't really object to these perambulations. Each move generally led to a few days of leave before he settled down again. And he had no time to get bored at home, for the day-time was spent in do-it-yourself jobs around the house. I must admit that Albert's efforts did improve the dingy, dirty interior considerably. In the evening, he would read the newspapers to find out how the war was progressing; that was the only means he had of knowing what war meant, apart from the separation from home. Or he would discuss what he would do when the war was over. Albert naturally wanted to return to London and continue being a milkman, while I had a strong desire to stay in my home town, especially as our sons were doing so well at school. Occasionally, if funds allowed, we would go to the local and drink beer. Even though the Canadians had left, the pubs were still lively and full of people in uniform, men on leave, home-guard, firemen and air-raid wardens. All found the pub a focal point where for an hour or two they could find mutual protection against their fears, in the same way as those people who had a faith, found it in the churches. The former dispensed a kind of liquid escapism, while the latter dispensed it spiritually.

In most local pubs there is always a 'character'. This individual, generally a male and a 'regular', by being oblivious to any snubs and rude remarks, eventually establishes himself as a personality. He has a collection of aphorisms, a veneer of intelligence and a ready laugh. Such a man was old Fred in our local. Long since a widower, with his son in Australia, the pub was his only link with life. I didn't mind him, but Albert couldn't stand it when, seeing Albert in Air Force uniform, he would start on about 'our heroic fighters in the skies', and how it was such men as them that kept us in England safe. I could well understand Albert's embarrassment as personally he was so remote from danger. In fact, it was more dangerous for him to be on leave, as we were still liable to have hit-and-run raids. The boys flatly refused to sleep in the 'Morrison shelter' in the living room. Albert and I used it at first but then we too took the risk of sleeping in a proper bed. I believe that to Albert it was the best part of his leave, having clean sheets and privacy to perform his ablutions.

On one of his leaves I asked Albert if he had noticed any change in our bedroom. Much to my mortification he replied that the only change he had noticed was the miserable amount of light, he couldn't see a darn thing, and what was the idea? Ever longing and hopeful for a more romantic approach to married life, I had put into effect something that I had recently read. When old Mr Borman died his sister had thrown out a pile of rather tattered books. Amongst them was a translation from Sanskrit on the art of love—a kind of Kama Sutra. Several pages described how the surroundings, the bower of sexual desire, should be arranged. Colours to excite the senses, music to eradicate all extraneous thoughts, and a dim and shadowy light to enhance one's charms.

As our bedroom bore not the faintest resemblance to this description, it was no easy task, with the limited means and material I had, to accomplish anything comparable, but I tried. The book went on to say that any sentient being would then, in this bower, be overcome with sensual desire. The book was a fairy-tale, or else Albert wasn't a sentient being. Nothing different materialised. Ah well! I was an early forerunner of those wives who are constantly being exhorted by modern magazines that if they want their marriage to be a success, they must work at it.

Although it was difficult to discuss the war with Albert, with my Mother the difficulty was to keep her off the subject. When Churchill and Roosevelt met at Casablanca at the beginning of 1943 to plan the final victory, my Mother, who admired both men, thought the war as good as won. Certainly she didn't believe it would last two more years. Shortly before D-Day I wrote to Albert with the glad news that his mother-in-law wished to tell him that he would soon be living a normal life. Albert was extremely indignant at this news. 'You ask your Mother, what does she think I am doing here? I *am* living a normal life. The only peculiarity is the way I am continually moved from camp to camp. I am leaving Topcliff next week, going to Handforth in Cheshire.'

My sons too thought it was rather odd the way that their Father was never allowed to stay in one place. Harry, who was already acquiring the superiority of his grammar school speech and education, to the fury of his brothers, said, 'Dad is getting to be like the Flying Dutchman. Except that there's nothing spectral about him.' As none of us knew a thing about the Flying Dutchman, we refrained from comment. But, as Albert wrote, the continual postings did at least demonstrate that the Air Force were aware of his existence, even if they couldn't quite decide just where his services would be of most help in winning the war.

'I'm at Handforth now, and not attached police any more, thank goodness. When you write, I am now known as 61 E.M.U.'

Here David, my middle son, who was as sharp as a razor with repartee, broke in, 'Tell Dad if he is an emu, not to be an ostrich; always protect his rear.' I did tell Albert but I don't think he got the point.

Albert continued, 'I thought I was on to a good thing here when I found that my bed in the Nissen hut was next to the door. More airy than being in the middle. I soon discovered why it was an empty bed. In the night it was swarming with earwigs. I can't stand the creatures. The job is easy enough, just checking vehicles in and out of camp. I won't be home for a while, leave's a bit tight here.'

Albert's next letter did nothing at all to cheer me up. I consigned his officers, and the powers-that-be, to perdition.

'What do you think, my love. I have now been sent to a huge WAAF camp in Wilmslow. There are only two men here, me and Jock. It's our job to stoke the boilers on eight different sites. We take it in turn to do night work. I'm here because the last man sent here did night work of a different kind. Instead of devoting his time merely to stoking the boilers, he was heating up a few of the WAAFs. But don't worry about me, love. I'll keep my mind strictly on the business. Besides, as you are always saying there's safety in numbers. Mind you, this is a cushy job, I wouldn't mind staying here for the duration. Jock and I have a decent hut to sleep in and our own washroom. One of the WAAFs brings our breakfast in and the other meals we have with them. Their boss is a terrifying woman. I'd sooner face a sergeant-major than have to be on the carpet in front of her. I don't think she even knows that there are two sexes.

'Poor old Jock got the shock of his life this morning. He still can't believe it's true, for like me he hasn't been out of England yet. He is being posted to Reykjavik, in Iceland. Just imagine if

I was sent there; I'd freeze to death.'

Naturally, my know-all children promptly wrote to their Father to assure him that he wouldn't freeze. Iceland was full of volcanoes and hot springs. It's Greenland that's icy.

Albert, usually very philosophical about his peripatetic life, was, for the first time, really angry about his next move—although I was considerably relieved.

'What do you think, Margaret, I have been sent back to Hand-forth. Now don't get alarmed. It's not because of anything I have done—apart from stoking the boilers. Yesterday we had a red-faced pot-bellied officer here from headquarters, and when he saw me he glared, but said nothing. Next thing I know there's an order come through, "What's a Grade I man doing on the WAAF camp?" And I'm packed back to Handforth, as though my continued presence was a danger. You ought to see the decrepit old replacement they have now.'

Well, I expect Albert was considered a danger by some impotent old big-wig. Albert looked the picture of health. Plenty of food and an easy life had done wonders for him, appearance-wise. And however much a man keeps his mind fixed on his wife and family, the propinquity of some hundreds of females, of whom at least one or two were ready with blandishments if the occasion warranted it, does present a certain problem. I could not pretend to be sorry that Albert no longer had female companionship. It's all very well to tell other people, 'I trust my husband implicitly.' I know that the spirit is willing, but the flesh is weak. Perhaps some of my antagonism was sour grapes, inasmuch as there was a distinct lack of males in my milieu. Still, I tried; having finished my course of geography, I was persuaded to join a drama class. Not that I needed much persuasion. Although it had been proved that I had no talent for painting, I was by no means convinced that I had no talent at all for art. In fact, such was my ebullient and optimistic nature, no sooner had I joined, than I had visions of myself as another Rachel, or a Sarah Bernhardt; so it was rather disconcerting to find that my contribution for the first few weeks was merely to arrange stage props. As usual with evening classes, there was a superabundance of women. We were eleven females, and only five males, of whom only one could be considered as a hero. The others were two spotty sixteen-year-olds and two men who had long since retired from active participation in life.

We were rehearsing a one-act play, a comedy called *Market Day at Little Pudford*. Although by the end of the term I had only progressed to walking on the stage and saying, 'It's a long way from Little Pudford,' nevertheless, I had learned the lines of the principal female's part—just in case. Especially as it involved kissing the only presentable man. Came the night, seats occupied by relatives and friends—all non-paying, principal female's Mother telephoned to say her daughter had 'flu, and must stay in bed. My big moment had arrived. I stepped forward nobly: 'I will fill the breach.' But where was the hero? Another telephone call. Hero had suddenly developed laryngitis, couldn't speak above a whisper. I must say, it was a let-down. Another female had to impersonate him, and she made a very realistic male as her frontal appendages were practically non-existent, although she had the build of a cart-horse. But I had to kiss her. It wasn't at all like kissing the hero.

When Albert came home on leave, I scrutinized him carefully to see if he was comparing me with the bevy of females he had so recently mixed with. But he looked the same, and everything else was the same. I suppose it had to be, otherwise I would have wanted to know what—or who—had changed him. Albert was full of his new job on the railway line.

'I ride up and down the lines in a train with Ministry of Works men checking that all the goods that have been sent from other camps are correct. I've learnt how to shunt the trucks, using a large pole with a hook on one end. It's not as easy as my cushy job on the WAAF camp, but it's more exciting.'

Who but a devoted wife like me would believe it was more exciting to ride up and down on a train than to be one of only two men amid hundreds of girls?

'I can tell you,' added Albert, 'the job calls for a certain amount of skill. I have to know just when to jump off the trucks, and they move pretty fast. I have to be alert and agile. It's not a job anybody can do, believe me; but I like it.'

Well, for heaven's sake. One would think trucking up and

down that single line track was comparable to riding the C.P.A. 'Don't get delusions of grandeur, Albert,' I warned him, 'and imagine that when you are demobbed you will be driving the Flying Scotsman.'

Chapter 14

I was doing two jobs now. One morning a week I worked for a very pleasant elderly lady, the only drawback being her two grossly overfed pug-dogs. The dislike was mutual at first, though eventually we learned to tolerate each other. Then on two mornings I worked for a Mr and Mrs Ecclestone. Her most noticeable feature was her flesh—she weighed about twelve stone—which was thick, creamy and pink. It seemed to have a life of its own. In contrast, poor Mr Ecclestone was as dry and desiccated as though some female Dracula had drained away his vital juices. Mrs Ecclestone was also, to put it mildly, a peculiar woman. Charlie was her third husband. In no time at all I was her confidante, hearing about most of her matrimonial adventures.

'My first husband was about fifty years old when we got married. Short, fat and half-bald, he had no interest in sex. Well, it stands to reason, doesn't it? There must have been something peculiar about him if he hadn't got booked before he was fifty.'

'Why did you marry him, then?'

'Well, I was thirty, and James was the first man who had asked me. I thought it was my last chance. Besides, he had a good job. I wasn't to know that he changed jobs as often as he changed his underpants. We only lived together six months.'

'What happened to him eventually?'

'Oh, he met a rich widow from India, and they went back there. He bought enough stuff with the money she gave him, you would have thought he was off to the Relief of Lucknow. About the only relief she'd ever get out of James; for sure she'd get none in bed. I went to a matrimonial agency for my second attempt at a life partner. I asked for a man about thirty.'

'Was he a success, Mrs Ecclestone?'

'It all depends what you mean by a success. I certainly succeeded in getting him to the registry office. But he was a dead loss for the reason I wanted him, and sixty if he was a day.'

'Why didn't you ask the Matrimonial Agency for another date?'

'He was the third one they had offered me. The other two were absolutely hopeless. The first one was called Ralph. I entertained him in my home on some half-dozen occasions. But he was so strange. Given to going into a kind of trance at most inconvenient moments.'

'How was it inconvenient?'

'Well, after plying him with drinks and soft music on the radio, I would try to establish a warmer relationship by gazing at him with liquid eyes and an air of expectancy. He would promptly assume a faraway vacant expression, as though he hadn't a clue what I meant or wanted.'

By this time I knew what Mrs Ecclestone's 'warmer relationship' entailed. I had known her too long to imagine that her idea of a warmer relationship just meant that her voice assumed a soft and alluring tone. No, what it meant was, that all that mass of creamy, living flesh would seem literally to ask to be fondled and caressed.

'The second man was more like a gorilla than a human being. He had hair everywhere.' I wondered how she knew. 'His strength was definitely the strength of ten, but assuredly it wasn't because his heart was pure. Now I've got Charlie. I tell everybody that I literally won him in a raffle. I bought a ticket for a charity "do". If you got the lucky number it entitled you to an evening and dinner with the organiser; that was Charlie. I won, though ever since I've had my doubts as to whether it was a lucky number. As you can see, Charlie's not exactly the top prize in a tombola. Our wedding night was a disaster. Five pounds I paid for a nightie, and no value received. I kept it on all the time. He hadn't a clue what to do. I was the first woman he had been to bed with. He'd lived for years with his mother and sister. I think he regarded me as an amalgam of a mother, sister and wife.'

Mr Ecclestone's version was the antithesis of hers. 'Mrs

Powell, going to bed with my wife, Clara, was more strenuous than being on army manoeuvres. I never knew what was coming next. In fact, I was reminded of my first day of army manoeuvres when I got hopelessly lost in the bed, and ended up on the carpet; fortunately, it had a thick pile.'

I had often wondered what those advertisements meant when they stated, 'carpet suitable for the bedroom'. Now I knew.

Mr and Mrs Ecclestone were always asking me to call them by their first names; but I seldom did this with people I worked for. However, when they took me out, I did manage to forget they were my employers. One evening they took me to the theatre, and afterwards on to a friend's house where the décor and atmosphere were pseudo-oriental. Heavy purple drapes, beaded curtains, an aroma of incense and people sitting on the floor. I really felt that I was living it up, especially when the host—there seemed to be no hostess—gave me a glass of a green concoction that tasted like nothing on earth. He said that it was his own invention and made one lose one's inhibitions. Judging by the appearance of some of the guests they had already lost more than their inhibitions.

Clara and Charlie had frequent rows, mostly occasioned by Charlie's passion for making articles of no use or aesthetic value. He had a mania for constructing things with matches and I had to bring all my used ones up for him. One day he made a 'Leaning Tower of Pisa' with unused matches. They had a row and Clara set fire to it. It really was a funny sight, lighted matches shooting out in all directions. We were frantically dashing around and diving under tables. I noticed that every time I went under a table Charlie followed me. I think he was more sexy than Clara made him out to be. But then, Clara averred, it was only having a row that got his adrenalin flowing so that he was able to perform. If that was true, Charlie must have put in overtime the day she burnt his Leaning Tower.

They let me use their bath, a pleasure that I much appreciated, though I was always somewhat apprehensive that either of them might look through the keyhole. I always hung a towel over it. I had no desire to join the collection of weird paintings that adorned the walls, all painted by Mrs Ecclestone.

The most irritating times were when she had her 'inner communications', her colour periods. She would lie on the bed and cover her eyes with coloured paper. This was supposed to induce different states of extra-sensory perception. If she used blue paper she floated on a sea of tranquillity; if orange, she was very soon transported to a violent world of strife and heat; while green would take her back to her childhood in Ireland. Whether any of this was true I never could be sure. At these times of suspended animation, nobody was allowed into the bedroom, not even Charlie. I used to welcome her blue periods, though Charlie was never in a good mood at these times, as it meant that Clara would be in a very sentimental mood about her Spanish Mother.

'My Mother was a beautiful woman and my Father loved her to distraction. Mother told me that their honeymoon in Ireland was literally out of this world. "Your Father and I were in a state of bliss the whole time, completely oblivious to the world about us." ' There would be reams of this mush, and poor Charlie would get very morose at his inability to compare favourably with such a sexual success as her Father. He would seek my company while Clara was shut in the bedroom, and console himself, with me, with a large brandy. 'Margaret, I have come to the conclusion that I am one of life's failures, a never-never person.'

This was uttered with a certain air of complacency as though there were some prestige attached to being a failure.

'The trouble with me, Margaret, is that I failed to meet the right woman. I'm afraid it's too late now.'

I am always slightly apprehensive when I hear remarks like that, in case they should imagine that I am the right woman. But Charlie merely required sympathy.

Maybe Mrs Ecclestone's Spanish Mother, Irish Father and Portuguese grandfather were the cause of her excursions into the astral world. I think her green periods were the most tedious. She would emerge from the bedroom and immediately launch into a stream of words about her childhood in Ireland, as though that country was alternately spewed out of Hell or a Heaven on earth.

'Bog Irish, that's what I was. Nine brothers and sisters in a two-roomed hut which we shared with the chickens and a pig at night.'

I thought at first that she meant a real pig, but she was referring to her Father. 'He made illicit whisky, a moon-shiner, as were most of our neighbours. But as he drank so much of his brew we were always half-starved. It was nothing but giving birth and dying in our home. Six brothers and sisters died, some as soon as they were born. My Father used to knock up the coffins out of old wood, and would always have the priest say the appropriate words over the grave. Then that same night he'd come home roaring drunk and knock up my Mother again.'

By now Clara would either continue, with tender reminiscences of her Mother completely forgotten, 'Bloody Irish bastard, and why the hell didn't my Mother stay in Spain,' or else we would hear, 'A lovely country Ireland, so fresh and green, such friendly people,' and for the rest of the day she would be everlastingly singing, 'I'll take you home again, Kathleen'.

There was never a dull moment working for the Ecclestones. It certainly compensated for the quietness of working for Mrs Sharman and the two pugs, Otto and Olaf—what names people give to their pets. Mrs Sharman was, for want of a better word, a really sweet person. Too old and frail to do all her own work, she was struggling to live on an inadequate fixed income, her only luxury the two dogs. I must admit, though they in no way resembled my idea of protectors, they would have died to protect Mrs Sharman.

Poor Clara Ecclestone had a sad, and sudden, end. A well-meaning friend, well I think she was only a friend, told Clara how much better she would look, and feel, if she lost some weight. In vain did Charlie protest that he loved her twelve stone, that he didn't want her to be slimmer. Though I should imagine it did present some problems in bed, he weighing in at about nine stone, against her twelve. Perhaps he practised passive resistance. Clara went off to a health farm, while I came in an extra morning to look after Charlie. Life was certainly more peaceful without Clara, but it lacked variety and excitement. Even after a couple of brandies Charlie wasn't exactly a sparkling raconteur. His conversation consisted mainly of how marvellous were his Mother and sister, and how they hadn't wanted him to marry Clara because Clara would change his personality.

'And has she done that, Charlie?' I enquired.

'Well, Margaret, let me say that I have lost some of my inherent convictions about married life. I always considered it a private contract between two persons. But my wife broadcasts far and wide most aspects of our marriage.'

Mrs Ecclestone wrote me a glowing account of the benefit that she was deriving from the health farm. 'All the poisons are being expelled from my system, I have masses of energy, have lost sixteen pounds in weight and feel ten years younger. Hope Charlie is not too miserable without me.' Of course, she really hoped that he was, if not exactly heart-broken, at least missing her. For, in spite of all the rows and verbal abuse, she really cared for Charlie in her own way. The day that she was due to leave the health farm, Charlie drove down there to collect her. On the way back, a car travelling much too fast crashed into them. The occupants of both cars were killed.

Albert was still shunting up and down on his miniature Canadian Pacific Railway; I don't believe it went faster than Stephenson's Rocket. Nevertheless, it was a step up, or so Albert said, from being on gate duty. He wasn't forever saluting officers, or what he imagined were officers, only to find afterwards that they weren't anybody important. Also, it was considerably better than being posted to Iceland; or so Albert thought. Actually, although I didn't wish for Albert's removal to such a remote place, there would have been a certain amount of prestige attached to having a husband in Iceland. I could visualise myself at the evening class informing an admiring audience—all my audiences were admiring—'My husband is out in Iceland, you know.' As Albert couldn't fly or service planes, it would have been difficult to give him an occupation out there. Perhaps he could have been helping the war effort by gathering that moss which is supposed to have food value. I just couldn't imagine myself saying, 'My husband's in Cheshire, doesn't know what an air-raid is. He rides a puffer train up and down and even shunts the trucks.'

When I told my Father all this, thinking to make him laugh, my Father, who was very fond of Albert, rather told me off. 'You mustn't denigrate Albert's service, Nell. What you must realise is that he is releasing some much younger man who can do a more spectacular job. Don't under-rate Albert's capabilities.'

Well, I never have done. I don't think that I under-rate the abilities of anybody—or mine either, come to that. Albert has often called me a female Walter Mitty, but a great many of my secret ambitions have come true, mainly because I willed them to.

One part of Albert's letter absolutely confirmed my Mother's opinion that the whole world was crazy and the brass-hats in England even more so. This letter was dated September 1944, so it wasn't long after D-Day.

Albert wrote, 'I wish you could have been here, love, to see what goes on.' I wondered why he didn't wish I was there for any other reason. Ah well! as Vi said, I've got a one-track mind. Albert went on: 'It was like something straight out of *Comic Cuts*. Once a week we have a pay parade and the O.C. decided that we had become apathetic and downright slovenly on this parade. So every day last week, in front of the empty table where the officers sit, we were marched up and down for an hour. You should have heard Jumbo Jones who was marching by my side. "Bloody lot of niminy nobs. Over there they're murdering each other. All they can think about here is bloody bull-shit. Left wheel, right wheel, when did you get your hair cut, Jones. I'd like to give them all a dose of bloody clap—if I could find anybody in this God-forsaken spot to service them!"

'Came pay-parade day. We are told it's got to be a pukka job. We march in perfect formation. At the end of the field there are four officers at the table. It's a gale-force wind, straight from Russia. They have actually got a strip of carpet in front of the table. As the first twelve men go to step on it the wind rolls the carpet up. Twelve men retire in disorder while carpet is laid down again with bricks at four corners. Twelve men advance again. Great blast of wind lifts cloth on table, money flies in all directions. Complete chaos as entire formation breaks ranks and dashes wildly over field in pursuit of money. What a loss to the paymaster that so much money got blown to the four winds. And what a peculiar sight it was that night to see faintly in the dark, figures crawling around the perimeter searching for notes they had hidden. I'd put my 10/- under a stone. There were high jinks that weekend. Jumbo Jones came back from the village covered in mud, but glory too. His sexual exploits far surpassed anything the others could relate. Don't worry about me. All I had was a couple of extra pints.'

I thought it very funny, and so did Dad, but my Mother fulminated at the ineptitude of the men in charge. 'There's your two brothers overseas, in danger all the time, there's John fighting fires in London, and all they can think of for the men to do where Albert is, is to march them up and down to collect their money. It's disgraceful, they ought to be shown up.'

I hastily informed Mother that neither I nor Albert considered the event warranted a national enquiry, and certainly not one set in motion by her writing a letter to the Government. My Mother was such a determined woman that she was perfectly capable of writing letters on the conduct of the war to half the heads of departments—and writing again if they didn't answer.

I went around to my friend Vi to tell her about Albert, but all was consternation and uproar. Our Rosie, the 'edicated' daughter, had discovered she was up the spout, in the pudding club, or in other words, in the family way. As her fiancé had been overseas for the last two years, this was awkward to say the least. Vi was ranting and raving, using all the expletives she knew—by no means a negligible amount. Not because Rosie had 'gone with a man', after all who could be expected to go without for two years, but because she hadn't taken precautions. Rosie was bawling her eyes out, 'Jack will kill me when he finds out. He'll never marry me now.'

When I told Rosie that as her Jack had been in France for two years he had probably been doing the same as her, she rounded on me furiously. 'My Jack's not like that. He writes me letters all the time. We were to be married the moment the war's over. Jack's got a good job to come home to. He never so much as looked at another girl.'

Well, you probably never so much as looked at another man while Jack was around, was my thought. But it was politic to be silent.

'How do you know that you are pregnant?' I asked Rosie. 'What symptoms have you got? You don't look any different to me.'

'I've got this book called, *How to become a Mother*, and it lists all the preliminary feelings. Morning sickness, going off food, dizzy attacks, having fads. I have all these symptoms.'

'Don't go by all that stuff, Rosie. You may only have constipation. It's like these advertisements for a patent medicine that say, "If you are suffering from any of the following ailments you need a course of Dr Pankey's Pallid Pills." You read through the list which details everything from flat feet to hydrophobia, and you think, my God, how have I lived so long without Dr Pankey's Pallid Pills, and immediately rush out to buy a box. After two boxes you feel so ill that you decide the list of complaints can be endured with more fortitude than his pills.'

This did at least make Rosie laugh. Then Dot Harris came in with a brilliant suggestion. Why not a hair of the dog that bit you? If you drink too much at night, another one in the morning clears your head. Dot had heard that if you had 'fallen', more of the same sexual treatment, if taken immediately, often did the trick. Unfortunately, Rosie had no hopes of more of the same treatment, at least not from the original source. He was a Canadian and had been sent overseas. But Rosie's dilemma was resolved by its turning out to be a false alarm. She must have had indigestion or some such ailment. Poor Rosie's fiancé never did come back from the war; he was killed three months before the finish. She married the Canadian and went to Calgary, Alberta, but couldn't stand the life there after London, left him and went to America. She drifted around from job to job and finally lost her life in one of those tornadoes to which they always give female names. There were many casualties of the war besides those that were killed by enemy action.

Chapter 15

Early in 1945, Albert wrote to say that he was being posted yet again, but he wasn't sure just where he was going. If Albert had stamps stuck on him for every time he was 'posted' he would have been a collector's item by now. 'I shan't be sorry to leave Handforth. I'm a bit cheesed off now that my job on the railway is finished. And it's mighty cold up here. Half the time the stoves are so temperamental they don't work. Or some lazy blighter whose turn it is to get the coke in hasn't bothered. And most of the original lot in the hut have been shifted somewhere else.'

But Albert's next letter was in a very different key. 'What do you know, Margaret. They are posting me to Faygate. I'll probably be able to get home every weekend. What a turn up for the book! What a celebration we'll have.'

How on earth Albert thought we could celebrate in our parlous financial state I had no idea. We certainly couldn't afford to go out for a meal, and the rations didn't allow for any Lucullan banquets at home.

Dear old Mrs Sharman, for whom I was still working—I had learnt to tolerate Otto and Olaf, as they had me—really came up trumps when I told her about Albert. She gave me a bottle of wine and a Christmas pudding that she'd had for over a year—both items were very good—and a tin of cream. She loved to talk about her childhood in the country, the lovely house, the woods around, nature in abundance. They had twelve servants in the house, as well as gardeners and grooms. 'The servants loved my Mother. She was so kind and understanding. My two sisters and I had a lady's-maid all to ourselves. It was the house-keeper they were in awe of, not Mother. When my eldest brother was twenty-one my Father gave a great party for all the villagers. We had huge trestle-tables laden with food, and dancing on the lawn. My parents and all of us children waited on the villagers. Those were grand days, Mrs Powell, but they will never come again.'

I received Albert's news about Faygate with mixed feelings. In theory, I know that I should have been delighted. But for over three years I had been the key figure in the home. I had written to the education authority for grants, paid all the bills, encouraged our sons to win scholarships—David was shortly to be the next one at the grammar school. Now I should have to delegate some of this responsibility, and I didn't want to. I liked being the one to make decisions for other people, as I had always made them for myself. Matters more practical had to be considered. If Albert was coming home every weekend, I needed more sheets, and I had no clothing coupons. Like many other mothers who were hard-up, I had sold a lot of my coupons. My principal source of clothing for myself and the boys was the Saturday jumble sales. As soon as we heard on the grape-vine that in so-and-so church hall there was to be a jumble sale, we mothers assembled in our hundreds, at least an hour before it opened. When it did we all surged in like stampeding elephants. It was the survival of the fittest. Sometimes, the vicar, if he could be heard above the din, would tell us that 'we'd be very welcome in church tomorrow; he hoped some of us would come'. Poor man, his hopes were very seldom realised. We were too busy sorting out our booty.

On that £3 sewing machine that Albert had bought me the year after we were married, I performed marvels of ingenuity. I unpicked trousers and remade them for the boys, I made new collars on shirts from the tails—and the new tail pieces were often any colour of the rainbow. But this didn't solve the problem of the sheets. However, by a stroke of luck, and from an unidentifiable source, I obtained a collection of light-coloured sacks, which perhaps had contained flour. Written across the sacks in black lettering was, 'Handle with care'. By boiling and bleaching I got the sacks nearly white, but couldn't eradicate the letters; they just turned a grey colour. It took about six sacks to make a sheet and an enormous amount of sewing and seams. The day that Albert came home I put one of these sheets on our bed, and turned it down so that right across the top it read 'Handle with care'. To this I pencilled, in front of 'handle', 'do not'.

I made a delicious meal of potato soup, with cream in it; kromeskies—they don't need much meat—and the Christmas pudding. We drank the wine with everything. I wanted to be all romantic and dine by candlelight. But Albert said it was daft; he'd much sooner see what he was eating. Finally, we retired to bed, and Albert saw the lettering on the sheet. He did laugh, but he didn't laugh any louder when he saw what I had added.

In more than one way it was beneficial to have Albert so near. For not only did the boys have a father again, it enabled me to settle down into matrimonial life by easy stages. I told Albert that he could invite one of the men from his hut to Sunday lunch, but Albert said he'd had enough of service men over the past years without carrying them into his private life.

I was already forced to make some alterations in *my* private life. I had to stop my friend Carrie from coming round every Sunday evening for help with all the competitions she entered. She did fashion, film stars, jingles and crosswords. As I was the only person she knew who possessed a dictionary, my help was necessary with the crosswords. These were the kind already filled in with a considerable amount of the words. Very easy to do, the snag being that there were about six alternative words for a lot of the clues. Only once did Carrie ever get it right. She waited in joyous anticipation for a prize in the region of £50. She got five shillings as, according to the paper, some hundreds of other entrants had also won—names and addresses provided if desired. I urged Carrie to send for this list; I'd have done so, but she wouldn't bother.

I still went out with my parents for a Saturday evening drink, but now Albert came too. Because he was always polite to my Mother, she had no idea that her very definite and loudly proclaimed opinions on the war irritated him beyond measure. Mother was so used to Dad, who loved her, and in any case was all for a quiet life, that she honestly didn't realise that at times Albert wished her anywhere but with us. She had a most annoying habit of enquiring of Albert just what good were all the men doing at the camp, merely idling away their time that could be put to better use. She was right, of course, and Albert knew she was. But it didn't endear Mother to him; Albert liked the life of the camp.

I'd given up the drama class. If I couldn't be the star I didn't want to be anybody. To be honest, no grief was shown at my departure. In fact, one catty female there, who had always tried to keep me in the background, muttered something like 'Now we can get on with the play without all those histrionics.' Professional jealousy—or in this case amateur jealousy—is a very sad thing. I was in a pottery class now. Marvel of marvels there were actually more men than women. Not young men, teeming with life, but nevertheless definitely persons of the male sex. Mr Jennings, who was about seventy, told me that he was a retired draughtsman. I couldn't believe that playing draughts had ever been a full-time or lucrative occupation, but I discovered that he meant he drew up documents and such like. Why couldn't he have said that at the start? This was his second year in pottery and he was a great help to me, showing me with endless patience the various techniques. Mind you, I suffered for this by going to his home. He and his wife were musical, Mrs Jennings playing the piano and he the clarinet. While drinking a minute glass of some syrupy concoction that passed for sherry, I had to register appreciation and enthusiasm for strange sounds that I had never heard before, pieces by Bach, Mahler, something in E flat major, all cacophony to me. Mrs Jennings proudly told me that 'dear Hubert came from a long line of musicians. Why, far back in the remote past, one of his ancestors played at court.' I endeavoured to assume an expression of awe, but as I was inwardly thinking that Mr Jennings was the end of the line as far as I was concerned, and I also had visions of a line busking outside the theatres, it was difficult to appear impressed.

Much to my chagrin, I was no more talented at pottery than I had been with the painting. Not the fault of our teacher. She was not only remarkably clever in the shapes she fashioned from the clay, she was also very knowledgeable about the art, telling us that it originated with the Egyptians in 5000 B.C. We heard about majolica, faience, slip-ware and jasper. But the potter's wheel never enabled me to turn out any object recognisable as such. I did make an ash-tray for Albert—not that he ever bothered to use those already scattered around—but it resembled nothing so much as a chunk of clay with a dent in the middle. Albert, who always praised my efforts, even if misguided, had to admit that perhaps pottery wasn't my métier.

So I reluctantly had to admit that I had no artistic talent; I couldn't paint, act or sculpt. As for flower arrangement, by the time I had made anything approaching a set piece, the flowers were half-dead. I now signed on for lectures on 'The great Russian Authors'. At least I had a head start there.

How marvellous it was that the war in Europe was nearly over. No longer had we to live in fear of bombs, destroying everything that made life worth living, family and friends. With Albert coming home so often now, our life was almost back to normal. The food rationing and clothing coupons didn't affect us all that much. We had never been able to afford to live luxuriously.

As usual, Albert had a soft job. I told him to make the best of it as Faygate would probably be the last of his Air Force service. He would soon have to get down to the unpalatable task of earning a living. The 'best years of his life' were coming to an end. I wondered too, if our conversation would come to an end, as most of it for the last four years had been about his life in camp. Faygate was no exception; most weekends at home were devoted to descriptions of the cushy life there.

'When I arrived at the camp,' said Albert, 'there seemed nothing of it after the huge place I had left. There were one or two broken-down and worn-out planes being guarded by erks in a similar condition. I had to report to the flight-sergeant. He was such a weedy man that his uniform must have been specially made for him. The weediness didn't affect his voice though, which was as loud as though he was talking through a megaphone.

'"You are L.A.C. Powell," he told me. "I don't know what that meant at Handforth. But here it means 'leading ablution cleaner'." Not on your life it doesn't, I thought. I've been in the Air Force too long to be a Joe Soap. But he is a decent fellow, and I think he likes me. I am attached headquarters, which means I don't do parades or guard duties. I seem to be fetching him cups of tea all the time. It's very funny here when we line up at the canteen. Everybody feels that the war is over, so that there's not much discipline, the men indulge in a bit of horse-play. Out comes our flight-sergeant, walks up and down the line roaring out, "I have never seen such a lot of slovenly boy-scouts." When he gets to me he breaks the line, makes the first half go to the back, and whispers to me to bring him a cup of tea as quickly as possible. And I'm not an "ablution cleaner", I'm a decorator. There is absolutely nothing to do, it's a farce being here at all. So in desperation they invent jobs. I am now painting the various huts, and officers' quarters. It passes the time and at least I have unlimited material. They don't buy the paint in pints like we have to. I laughed fit to burst this morning. Three of the men were detailed to repaint the fire extinguishers. When they had finished they stood all these lovely bright red objects on the field to dry. Came a terrific gust of wind which blew them over and dirt and grass were stuck all over the wet paint. Just to see the men's faces was enough to make a cat laugh. Their sergeant was furious and threatened to put me on guard duty for grinning; but he has no authority over headquarters staff.'

Albert 'found' an old bicycle that had been left on the camp for the last two years. Probably the airman who left it never had the chance to come back. Albert rode it all the way home, 26 miles. It nearly killed him. He fully intended to ride the bicycle back one weekend, but kept postponing the ordeal until it was too late, the war had ended. For years afterwards he rode that old machine.

May 1945, and the war in Europe was over. But there were no scenes of wild rejoicing such as occurred on Armistice Day, 1918. This Second World War, which had involved civilians, had for the first time brought home to them just what the horrors of total war could mean. After six years of violence and terror, not many people felt like singing and dancing.

Albert thought that he would very soon be demobbed, but it was November before he, perhaps reluctantly, left the Air Force, and a life he would never again experience. Albert's last anecdote of his service life even made our boys laugh—and me too, although I'd heard so many.

'We have the Air Force regiment stationed at Faygate, and a smart lot of men they are. But when it was known that a brass hat was coming to inspect the camp before it folded up, the sergeant decided that the detachment assigned to escort the brass hat from the train to camp wasn't smart enough. Faygate Station is just at the back of the camp, and for a whole week this detachment have been drilled for their job of marching to the Station, waiting for the brass hat to alight, then escorting him to camp. They were so well drilled that they moved as one man. Came the great day; he was due to arrive at noon. At ten o'clock the sergeant musters his detachment for one last drill. They march up the lane, round the perimeter of the camp and into camp. There they find the brass hat. While they were up the lane he had come in on the ten o'clock train and just walked in the back way on his own. There wasn't even a guard to challenge him; a fact that gave the brass hat a very good idea of the efficiency of this camp. As for what the detachment said! Well, the sergeant already had a red face, his ears must have been burning too.'

Albert went back to Cardington to collect his demob suit, the possession of which doubled the contents of his wardrobe. Certainly was no Savile Row model, but at least the wind didn't blow through it as easily as it did through the suit he had left behind for service uniform.

Chapter 16

Now came the serious discussion: what was he going to do as a civilian? Naturally enough, now that service life was no more, Albert wanted to return to the life he had known before—a life in which we had all been reasonably happy. Our sons had no inclinations one way or the other. Although two of them were at the grammar school, it would be no wrench for them to leave and move back to London. But I dreaded the prospect of returning and searching for rooms. It had been difficult enough before the war, when the three boys were small. Who would let us have three rooms, especially now that so many houses were in ruins? Here in Hove, we lived in a whole house; once we had shut our front door, no stranger could enter. The lack of hot water, bathroom, and indoor sanitation was nothing, for we had never had those luxuries. Nevertheless, Albert was the breadwinner. He it was who had to support us. If he wanted to return to the Express Dairy, then of course he must do so. He went to the head office in London. They offered him a milk-round with a considerably higher wage than when he left. Albert stayed up there two days searching for somewhere to live. It was a hopeless task. There literally was nothing in the way of unfurnished rooms. Although the proffered wage was higher, it wasn't enough for Albert to go into lodgings up there, and just see us at weekends. Very unwillingly he decided we must remain in Hove. I endeavoured to mitigate his disappointment, though inwardly overjoyed that we were not going to live in London.

I listed all the advantages, though I omitted to mention the sea as I knew that Albert would never go near it.

'The air is cleaner, there's less noise, plenty of shops. You'll get to like it, Albert. Why, you might even get to like Mother; she will grow on you.'

Albert muttered some extremely uncomplimentary remarks on the type of growth that would be, but realised also that Hove was where his home was—if not his heart. We listed his assets; two suits, gratuity money, ability to do a milk-round, be a butcher or painter's labourer—although the last job was doubtful as Albert couldn't climb high ladders. We could see that his market value was not going to earn a fortune, but we would live. I could continue to work.

My Father was happy that we were not leaving Hove, and although Mother gave no visible sign of rejoicing, I believe that she too was glad that we would be near.

The return to power of the Labour Party in the election of 1945 astounded a great many people, and in particular my Mother. She just could not believe that Churchill, from being a national hero, had become an outcast again. Individually, he was still respected, even venerated, but en masse the people had had enough. They wanted no more of 'blood, tears, toil and sweat'. Churchill had been the man of the moment, but that moment was no more. If he had crossed the floor to become a Labour leader, no doubt that party would have been returned with an even larger majority. The people blamed the Tory government of Stanley Baldwin in the thirties, with its appeasement policy, for the evils of 1939-1945. They chose not to remember that they would have execrated any government that took them to war, as they did in 1939.

I think that the 1945 election generated more enthusiasm and excitement than any I have known. Very few were apathetic about voting. For a while we had the illusion that we really had some say in the running of the country. Men and women knocked on our door to solicit our votes. With endless patience they listened to our version of how the country should be run, as though they were fascinated that such political erudition could emanate from so unlikely a source. Alas! When they had been elected—or beaten—the knocking ceased, never to be heard or seen again until the next election.

My dear Dad had lost all interest in the Labour Party, which was just as well for his peace of mind, as Mother was vociferous enough for both. I was the recipient of most of her fulminations.

'To think, Nell, that after all Winston had done, his Party

should have been rejected. Where has loyalty gone? Why, if it hadn't been for him, we might have been governed by Hitler. It would serve some of those renegades right too. You mark my words, this Labour government will turn out as ineffective as was Ramsay MacDonald's.'

Albert, as usual, took no interest at all in who came into power; assuming, perhaps with truth, that it would not make the slightest difference to his eventual civilian job and wage packet. He and my Father put up a passive resistance to Mother's belligerency. But what a fortunate family we were, with Albert in even better shape than before he was called-up, and my three brothers unscathed. The youngest, Donald, who went to war a boy of eighteen, was now at twenty-four a man and, though physically in good shape, was mentally never again the laughing and carefree brother that I loved. He had seen and experienced too many horrors in those six years.

Albert was now a removal man. He still wasn't sure how or why he got this job, although I reminded him, with great frequency, that it was the best of the only two he was offered by the Labour Exchange. The other job was shovelling coke in the gas works. He could have been a milk roundsman, but Albert was determined that if he couldn't be a milkman in London, he most assuredly would not be one in Hove at considerably less wages. The munificent weekly payment that he received for this removal job with its hard work and erratic hours was four guineas.

One would have thought it impossible that adults and three growing boys could have been fed, clothed and housed on this meagre sum. But it was possible, and we all had good health. Albert would have liked me to give up my daily jobs, although he could see that the extra pound or two coming in did provide us with an occasional evening out. There was now a falling off in the glut of daily work available. So many mothers, who had been in factories and offices connected with war work, were now thrown on the market and looking for a civilian job. My dear Mrs Sharman had died. The funeral was attended by five distant relations, one of whom took Otto and Olaf to the vet to be also removed from life. Though I really believe that they would have died of grief, anyway, for they would not eat.

When I went out to work our diet was considerably more varied. Otherwise we ate quantities of boiled rice, porridge and herrings, such food as was approved by nutritional experts. Even Lord Horder, that determined opponent of the Health Service, had affirmed this food to be 'palatable and satisfying', though no doubt he and the nutritional experts seldom, if ever, needed such nutrition. As in my life below stairs, the working class obviously needed their appetites satisfied, not titillated.

I saw in the Situations Vacant column of our local paper that a firm was requiring pollsters, no experience necessary, but tact and patience needed. As I considered that I had these two attributes in abundance, I wrote for an interview. Such was the dearth of applicants that I believe I would have got the job with no qualifications of any kind. It was to conduct an enquiry on whether the householder already had central heating, or was thinking of having it. Did they favour solid fuel, gas, electricity or oil? Were they going to 'do-it-themselves' or employ an experienced firm? What a job it was. And what a vast army of 'don't knows'. At least the don't knows were honest. How could they know? They hadn't studied the relative merits of the different fuels; they certainly hadn't yet mastered the techniques of installation; above all they didn't know whether they could afford it. I found it an exhausting, interesting and occasionally hilarious business, this knocking on doors. We six pollsters each had our selected areas, but of course it was useless to knock on some doors where they were obviously too poor. However, one sometimes made mistakes in weighing up people's affluence. Many of the householders had no intention, then or at any time, of having central heating; but they were not averse to wasting my time on a prolonged discussion of any other subject. Somebody to talk to was all they needed. On one occasion, with my black plastic-covered notebook at the ready, I was extremely gratified to be immediately invited in before I had spoken a word. It was nearly five minutes before I discerned, in the woman's non-stop flow of words, that she had assumed I was from the Welfare.

There were don't knows, don't cares and many that simply

told me to 'get lost', or 'knotted'. After the first week my note-book registered thirty don't knows, five definite opinions, five would like to know more, and ten miscellaneous. These last included the man who said he could tell that I could provide all the central heating he needed; the man who said, 'Come in and I'll show you mine'; and the man who said he was anxious to know more, and only just in time did I discover what he desired to know more of. One formidable woman immediately bawled out, 'Fred, come here,' and when Fred arrived she said, 'Look at this. Bloody government snooper trying to find out if we can afford central heating. What we want is a bloody lavatory indoors. My Fred's like to catch his bloody death of cold sitting out there at night. It's already done his insides a mortal injury.' By the look of him it hadn't done much for his outside. 'Go and snoop on that bloody snob over the road with her ding-dong door bell, and her bloody tax-dodging old man.' Knowing it would be useless to explain that it was a private survey, I hastily departed. The job lasted six weeks. I wasn't too sorry when the end came, and Albert was definitely relieved. Even the bowd-lerised version of my exploits had him worried.

Although Albert's job was poorly paid, he was enjoying the work, especially when he was on a job with the horses. This old established firm still used two horses, and some of their old customers asked for them when they were moving home. Natur-ally, the arrival and departure were much slower than with the motor pantechnicon, but the customers seemed to imagine that along with the old-fashioned method of travel, went old-fashioned and deferential men. Unfortunately, the oldest customers were generally the least wealthy, so could not afford to tip the men in a munificent way. Albert came home one evening laughing —the other men were furious—because they had been on a removal job that took three days and eight men. When they had finished, the dear old lady handed the foreman a £1 note saying, 'You have all been such good workers, that's to share between you.' It worked out at 2/6d each and we had a hilarious evening trying to decide how to spend this magnificent gift. Finally we had two ninepenny seats in the cinema and a quick dash in and out of the pub. She had also told the men to help themselves to cigarettes, but they were Egyptian. Albert brought back half a dozen for me. I was smoking one in the cinema and indulging in fantasies of climbing the Pyramids or asking unanswerable questions of the Sphinx, when suddenly I heard rude remarks from the row behind us about the horrible smell. Indignantly, I said to Albert, 'Look round and see who it is.' He looked round and said, 'It's two men, love, and they're bigger than me.'

'In that case, out goes the cigarette. Can't afford to have the bread-winner damaged.'

One of his removal jobs was to take a family of six children from a huge old rambling house to one of the new-fangled open plan houses. The wife reckoned it would be labour-saving. But how so? From having one or two untidy rooms, on which one could shut the doors, with open plan the whole place is mucky and untidy. The architects and designers prate about the advantages of community living, having the family always under your eye, the children around you. But a wife and mother surely doesn't want the children continually around her. Far better for her peace of mind to have the family pursuing their interests in separate rooms. Then there are the open plan cooking smells that permeate the whole house, and the enormous picture-windows that alternately over-heat and dazzle one with the sun, or give a vista of soggy rain-swept landscape. I'm for keeping the outdoors where it belongs. Glass houses are for raising plants, not humans.

My Mother, forever perusing the newspapers, mainly for ammunition for her arguments, was becoming increasingly pessimistic about life, and told us so with monotonous regularity.

'You know, the U.N.O. will be no more effective in preventing war than was the old League. Those Russians will never be the same as us. They have the Cominform; they've taken over Czechoslovakia, and now they've blocked off Berlin and we have to feed it. If Churchill had been Prime Minister, it would never have happened. He wouldn't have been so spineless.'

Useless to point out to Mother that far worse events might have occurred under Churchill. In any case the public were not yet disillusioned with the Labour Party. Attlee and Bevin in particular were held in high esteem. This, in spite of the farcical Tanganyika ground nut scheme. As some wit wrote, 'The humble monkey nut has certainly made a monkey out of our government.'

I'd taken a job in what the proprietors called a Private Hotel, but what in reality was nothing more than a boarding house. It was owned, and chiefly run, by a Mr and Miss Porter, brother and sister. It was difficult to believe they were related, so unlike were they. Miss Porter was a keep-fit fanatic. Every morning at six a.m., come rain or shine, she would rise, put on a thick black battle dress, and trot up to the recreation ground, there to jog-trot round and round for half-an-hour. I once saw her in this battle dress; believe me, it was really something. Miss Porter was five feet ten inches tall and broad to match. It would have been a bold or a very foolhardy man who had ideas of assaulting her. This constant battle with the elements, though it may have been good for her health, had done nothing for her skin. Her face was generally bright red and looked as tough and grainy as old leather. Nevertheless, at sixty years old she looked remarkably fit, so much so that I was seized with the idea of joining a keep-fit class—not for me the public exhibition of exercise. I tried to persuade Albert to join, but the very idea of standing around wearing only a pair of shorts was enough to put him off. He flatly refused to display his manly charms. Besides, he reckoned that he got enough exercise humping around colossal wardrobes and grand pianos. Mr Porter was of the same opinion as Albert, for which I didn't blame him. His meagre, short figure was definitely not one of his assets. The brother and sister got on remarkably well considering Miss Porter's somewhat disconcerting character. The first morning I was there she told me, with alarming candour:

'It's all right, Mrs Powell, to go into my brother's room while he is in bed. Though he's a nice person, he's always been a fairy. The only female he ever loved was our Mother, who doted on him to the exclusion of her two daughters. None of us ever got married. My sister died in some remote place abroad where she went as a missionary. I always told her there were enough souls to save here, but she was determined to save our black brothers. She fell off a suspension bridge. I'm surprised that she ever went on it as the word "suspended" always filled her with horror from the day her bank suspended payment. It's true that she had only £7 9s 6d in her account, but it was the principle of the matter. That a bank could "suspend" and lose people's money meant that nothing was safe in England. She was the only woman among all those uncivilised people living in that steaming heat. But none of the men ever tried to rape her.'

A fact that didn't surprise me if the sister was anything like this Miss Porter.

It was never dull working in a boarding house. Miss Porter, as well as her regular summer visitors—or paying guests, as she preferred to call them—had three permanent boarders. Two were widows, and the third, a sprightly old man, was perpetually trying to escape their attentions. Mr Trowbridge had two pre-occupations in his life: his writing of the definitive History of England, beside which Gibbon's *Decline and Fall* would be as a mere tract, and his hernia. This last prevented poor Horace from sitting for long periods, so much of his epic had to be compiled walking around the room. Many and weird were the contrivances he had bought for the relief of his hernia. I used to feel highly embarrassed at having to shift these objects while doing his room, but Horace took no notice. In fact, with a complete lack of diffidence he would explain to me just how they all worked.

'You know, Mrs Powell, my hernia was caused by constipation. And that was caused by my Mother dosing us with syrup of figs or brimstone and treacle. At the end our functions didn't work naturally. What untold harm one's parents can do! Mother ruined us physically and Father ruined us financially. He always had grandiose ideas for "getting rich quick". He invented a gambling system which, if one stuck to it long enough, was infallible. Unfortunately, he didn't have the time to stick to it long enough, being forcibly removed by the law at the instigation of his creditors. Though, as my Mother bitterly complained, "how can he pay off his debts while in prison?" He was quite happy there. In fact he was glad to be free of Mother's wrath and we collected his share. When he came out of prison he went abroad without even a goodbye to his ever-loving wife and five snivelling children. We didn't miss him, and Mother parcelled us out, all except me, the youngest, among relatives. I've nothing against marriage, Mrs Powell, it's a fine institution I'm sure, but not for me. Those two charming ladies next door who are looking for another husband—Mrs Chatterton's already seen two off—simply terrify me. Besides, I have my life's work to do.'

As Mr Trowbridge had not received a university education, I wondered how he could tackle such a mammoth task, how he knew what books to read. I didn't realise then that, having already been working on it for ten years, he would never finish. For if he did, he too would finish, his reason for living gone.

Mrs Chatterton, she who had outlived two husbands, would never have a hope in hell of adding Horace to the number. What she would have done with his collection of rupture-containers, I don't know. Rhoda Chatterton had once been the prettiest deb of the year, and even now with her peroxided hair, faded blue eyes and ample form, it was possible to see some trace of that erstwhile kittenish charm. Unfortunately, Rhoda seemed unable to realise that the time for kittenish ways had long since passed her by. She dressed in an ingénue style, used excessive make-up, too frequently gave a tinkling laugh and endeavoured to look coy.

There was no lack of conversation in our house now. I related the idiosyncrasies of the boarders and Albert did the same for his removal customers; not exactly intellectual conversation, but then very hard physical work is not conducive to an alert brain. Our sons at the grammar school could never understand this mental apathy, but then all they had to do was soak up knowledge, a very pleasurable occupation. Instead of 'tales of Air Force life', we now had 'tales of a removal man'. Unfortunately, they had nothing in common with the *Decameron*, and they went on considerably longer.

'You know, Margaret, when we are out on a job, we have 2/- road money, that's for a midday meal, and 4/6 a night sleeping out money. If they have unloaded the furniture van the men sleep in it, and save their 4/6. I must have some bedding, for every man has his own roll of it hidden in the warehouse. When they know that they are going to be away for a night or two, they surreptitiously sneak their bedding into the van—they are not supposed to sleep in it. It's pretty uncomfortable on the floor, but I don't mind; it reminds me of our huts in the Air Force.'

On one occasion he came back from three nights away full of the good time he'd had.

'We moved this stockbroker, Mr Beaumont, from Hove to up north. He and his wife followed us in their car with a caravan attached, stuffed with food and drink. We stopped for a meal by a lovely lake. Mrs Beaumont set up tables and we all sat down to a cold collation, with wine. Fortunately our driver was a teetotaller. When we finally arrived, late in the evening, we laid our bedding on the floor of the empty house; they slept in their caravan. Mr Beaumont took the four of us down to the village pub. His family had lived in the village for donkey's years, and we were treated like royalty. The following morning he even lent us his car to get a breakfast in the village. What a nice couple they were; I'd like to work for them permanently. They said that they'd never had such a good job done before. Funny thing was, they thought that *I* was the foreman and gave me the tip to share.'

By the end of this recital Albert's audience of four was reduced to one. The boys had silently departed. I quite enjoyed this saga of how the well-to-do live, but was mainly interested in the amount of the tip he collected. I was firmly convinced that Albert halved this before disclosing the amount. Not that I blamed him, or minded. After a hard week he had very little money of his own for cigarettes. If he had collected a few tips he always took me out for an evening. On one occasion he brought home a kitten. They were moving a lady who bred pedigree cats; she had twenty of them. Unfortunately, one of their cats had been overcome with a desire to find her own mate, and somehow escaped from the cattery. The resultant litter of kittens, Albert said, was a truly wonderful sight, all the colours of the rainbow. This lady was trying to dispose of the motley collection, so, on being assured it was a male, Albert brought one back that had patches of black, white and ginger. We christened it 'Cat', as we had the previous one. After all, when we called

'Cat, Cat', he came running just as if we had called him Marmaduke. I was quite pleased to have a cat again, especially as my youngest son was keeping mice. Or rather, he was endeavouring to keep them. They chewed their way out of their boxes in the coal-shed with alarming rapidity. Phillip could never seem to determine their gender. Mice must be always copulating—I suppose they have nothing else to do—for they multiplied like lightning. He had one huge ginger mouse with pink eyes; it looked more like a rat to me. These confounded tame mice escaped from the coal shed and came into the kitchen. I'd find them on the draining board, gas-stove and floor. They couldn't eat the food, as we had always consumed that overnight. Our kitten, Cat, had the time of his life rushing after these rodents, which he consumed with relish, much to the fury of our son. Well, as I pointed out, poor Cat didn't live a life of luxury in our house. Cat grew into a quite handsome animal, and a very sagacious one. He needed to be to survive the rigours of living with us. Cat would eat anything and everything. One of his favourite dishes was hot Oxo with bread in it. Oxo cubes were only a penny each and I made one do for twice. One day Cat came in with a whole fresh herring in his mouth; heaven knows where he had found it, or filched it. He laid it reverently on the floor and gazed at us for approbation. The boys were all for us having it for tea, but as I pointed out, not only was one herring impossible to divide among five people, but we couldn't deprive Cat of his prize. I really liked Cat and I think he liked me, because I treated him with the respect he deserved. Occasionally, he would condescend to sit on my lap, but Cat was a very aloof and independent animal. When he was sitting in his own special place, that meant he wanted to be left alone. I considered that Cat was clever, though our sons derided this, saying, 'What are his accomplishments? He can take the laces out of our shoes, tear newspapers to shreds, dash madly after flies—which he never catches—and claw the furniture. Is that being clever?'

I immediately and indignantly defended Cat. 'What about when he rattles the door handle to be let out; waits behind the door for the milkman; puts his paw in the food to see if it's too hot, and sits on the draining board when he wants water to drink. Not clever indeed!'

Our son Phillip was not alone in being deceived by genders. I came home from work one day to discover that Cat had changed from a 'He' to a 'She', and was now a proud mother. She'd got her litter in my duster box too, much to my annoyance. If I had known that all that caterwauling in our yard was caused by Cat, I'd have been out there like a shot.

I was all set to make Mr Trowbridge laugh at this incident the next morning, only to find he was full of a far more exciting affair. As I was walking to the house I saw an ambulance just moving off. On enquiring of my 'male' employer why, he started to giggle:

'Oh, Margaret, you've missed a sight for sore eyes. One of our regular summer boarders, Mr Campion, walked into the break-fast room this morning stark naked. He strolled in for all the world as though he was walking along the sea-front, and sat down next to Mrs Chatterton. You should have seen her face; you'd have thought it was the first time she had seen a man naked. Come to that, perhaps it was. Maybe her long-departed husbands died from sheer frustration at never being able to display their vitality in the daylight. You can tell that Mrs Chat-terton was too refined for vulgar copulation. My sister never turned a hair, and she a spinster too. She calmly picked up a tablecloth and draped it around Mr Campion, took his hand and led him up to his room. He went like a lamb when the ambulance arrived.' When I went in to do Mr Trowbridge's room, he too was full of the unexpected excitement. Momen-tarily he'd even forgotten his hernia, and the History of England. 'I reckon it was the change of diet that caused Jack Campion's aberration. For years we have always had shepherd's pie on a Monday evening. We know what to expect, and we like it. Last night, without a word of warning, roast chicken was served. We couldn't believe it was true. It was enough to send anybody off balance. One good thing, Mrs Powell, the shock will put Rhoda Chatterton off seeing me as a life-partner, at least for a while. It's so long a time since she's seen the fundamental male, she had forgotten how gross we are.'

I couldn't help feeling that any woman would have to be desperate to want close contact with Mr Trowbridge and his hernia contraptions.

I came home all agog to relate this to Albert, only to find that he'd left a note, 'Off to Cornwall, see you in five days.' One of the irritating things to me about this job was that the men were never told until the last minute who was going to be on a particular van. Anybody would imagine that the firm were afraid the men would be making arrangements for hi-jacking. And what a nice life for Albert. I'm stuck at home with three sons, a job in a boarding house and great Russian literature to study in the evening, while he's cavorting down to Cornwall. The inequalities of life are truly appalling. When he came back I'd have nothing of interest to discuss because I had seen nobody and done nothing except be a housewife. I knew that Albert wouldn't be interested in my literature studies; he cared only for Westerns, with not more than six characters, hero, heroine, sheriff and three baddies.

Sure enough, when Albert returned, he was full of the good time they'd had, what a super job it had been.

'When we heard that we were moving a vicar, we all looked at each other with no joy. It's murder as a rule at a vicarage. Full of all the old junk accumulated over years, hundreds of knick-knacks, and a general feeling that one must speak in hushed voices being so near to the higher life. But this vicar wasn't a bit like that, he was real matey.'

'I can just see him, Albert. One of those really trendy men who very soon realised that his removal men were secular, not spiritual. Probably he tells his congregation not to worry if they cannot see the Gospel as a way to salvation. It's also a way to live for, and enjoy, their material life and possessions. What these really with-it clergymen endeavour to impart, is not to worry too much about attaining the Kingdom of Heaven; the Bible has to be re-interpreted in the light of new events.'

But Albert protested that this vicar wasn't a bit like that.

'You could tell, by the way that his parishioners kept calling in with little farewell gifts, that they really loved him. He'd been sent from Scotland a bottle of real malt whisky which he opened for us. Of course, we didn't appreciate an unblended one, nevertheless two generous tots went down very well. I got extra as I drank our driver's share. By the time we had nearly finished the bottle I think the vicar got a bit bewildered by the variety of names he had acquired. We addressed him at different times as Mr, Sir, Rev., Father, and old Fred even went as far as Your Grace. But what a change for the Vicar. From Brighton to this remote village in Cornwall, miles from a decent-sized town. When we finally left, he said that he couldn't thank us enough for all our help. We'd laid the carpets, hung pictures and put up the beds. He really had tears in his eyes when he said goodbye to us. What a very good man to meet on a job.'

I reckon the tears in his eyes were grief at leaving Brighton and being stuck down in a vicarage miles from nowhere; not grief at parting from six removal men.

Chapter 17

Nineteen-fifty, the general elections were over, and my Mother jubilant that the Labour Party were not as popular. Although still in power, they had no overwhelming majority. This election had not generated such fierce political arguments as the previous one, although the whole machinery of organisation had been used. In 1950 we were spared the television broadcasts which now bring aspiring, if not inspiring, candidates into one's home. We had public opinion polls, and my sympathy went out to the young woman who, not knowing my Mother, asked for her opinion. Mother, who for years had been giving us her un-solicited opinions, was delighted actually to be asked to reach a wider audience. It took Mother half-an-hour; even then she hadn't finished, but the young lady had. I think she had finished for ever.

The newspapers, those guardians of the truth and purveyors of 'objective' news, still managed to print reams of information, good or bad, according to which party they favoured. I used to think that it must be marvellous to be a Press Lord and have the power to change public opinion. But now I do not believe that people's opinions are changed so easily. They listen and read, but most have already decided. Way back in the thirties Mr Baldwin had stated, 'The papers conducted by Lord Beaverbrook and Lord Rothermere are engines of propaganda for the constantly changing policies, likes and dislikes of the two men.' He may have been right, but I do not believe that they had the power to change, or often did change, the likes and policies of their readers.

I had managed to get Albert to the polling station; thereafter his interest became, as usual, non-existent. Some years later, my sister Pat and I joined a political association. I think we both visualised ourselves as contributing valued opinions on how the Party should be run, even perhaps as possible candidates for a future election. As I told Pat, I could speak twice as fast as she could, and also had a propensity to use long, portmanteau and unintelligible words, so my chances were far greater than hers. We did not remain members for long. I had always assumed that the whole aim and object of a discussion was to examine the topic from all angles, with an open mind. But these people already had a fixed opinion; no amount of lucid or logical talk would ever make them change.

Albert, who before we joined had told us it was a waste of time, time which would be better spent on entertaining our respective husbands, with great magnanimity forbore from saying, 'I told you so.' In any case he was far more concerned with his immediate task, removal of the home of an Air Force officer. From the manner in which Albert became so nostalgic about his own service life, and his enthusiasm for this officer, I assumed that he knew him well, only to discover that the connection was tenuous; they had both served, on different occasions, on the same post. Mind you, I too became considerably more interested when I heard Albert continue with 'He's a real gentleman. If we make a good job of his removal he is going to give us two pounds each on top of the normal tip that he would have given. I'm acting foreman on this job; thank heaven I've got a decent crew.'

Two pounds extra money; what a lovely sum. Tantalising visions of dress material, hat or shoes, floated before my eyes. For although during the ten years Albert had worked at this job, he'd had a few 6/- rises, his wages were still very meagre. The cost of living was rising slowly; with the increase in rates our rent was now 25/- per week instead of the £1 we had started with.

It rather annoyed me, though not Albert, when he was made temporary acting foreman on a job, for with the increased responsibility went no increase in wage. But Albert really liked the open-air life, the travelling around, every day a different place, another home. He came back after three days from the Air Force officer's removal, full of reminiscences of his service life. This officer and

Albert had discussed the various aspects of life in wartime.

'What war was that, Albert? As far as I know you were never within miles of one, never had an air-raid even.'

Albert ignored all this; it wasn't a topic to be frivolous about in his opinion.

'You know, Margaret, he was a real gentleman, absolutely no side to him. We yarned all the evening in the pub as though we were on equal terms. It was simply great being able to go over old times. If I had been younger I really believe I would have stayed in the Air Force in peace time. What a grand lot of chaps I met.'

Our sons greeted all this with regrettable lack of filial respect. The youngest groaned, 'Oh, Dad, not again! Ad infinitum, ad nauseam'—all Greek to Albert. But our eldest, on vacation from his university, was horrified at his father's assumption that class distinction was right. 'What do you mean Dad, "he spoke as though you were on equal terms"? You are; he's not above you.'

Our sons could not understand how their Father could take pride in his work. To them it was just an unskilled job, with meagre rates of pay. But Albert really enjoyed handling lovely things—such opportunities were conspicuously lacking in our home, apart from me, of course. Albert was now a skilful packer of Spode, Wedgwood and Crown Derby. He handled Chippendale and rare old French furniture, and reverently removed valuable paintings. Unlike some of the gang, Albert never envied the people who owned such treasures. He sympathised with his customers when increased taxation made them part with family heirlooms.

Like most ambitious parents, we wanted our sons to have a better chance in life than we'd had. We considered that their education would help to bridge the gaps between the haves and the have-nots—at least intellectually. The eldest and youngest began to feel at home in both worlds. Our middle son, David, was the exception. Mixing with well-to-do boys he became first uneasy and then really concerned about the inequalities of life, that some starved while others feasted, that some lived in revolting overcrowded slums, while others owned two or three houses. It really hurt him that his Father worked so hard for so little, and that I went out to 'do' for people. He found it difficult to believe that neither of us minded, that we enjoyed life. I would try to reassure him, 'But David, Dad and I are used to having very little money, we really don't mind. It's not all work, you know. We enjoy our occasional outings to the theatre or cinema.'

'Oh Mum! I'll never, ever, forget when we were at the grammar school and you and Dad, in spite of the grants, just couldn't afford to buy us sports gear. I know it grieved you so. Neither of you spoke about it, and you tried your best to hide the lack of money. But I know; for every stair-tread creaked, "No money, no money", every opening door brought in "No money, no money".'

Poor David, for such a sensitive and vulnerable nature life was very hard to live, and always would be.

While they were still studying, so was I. I had completed my course on 'Great Russian Authors' and received high praise for an essay in which I had really gone to town. I wrote,

'In Dostoevsky's novels, drama and suspense are increased by the underlying sense of despair and inevitable doom. Tolstoy's *Kreutzer Sonata*, though not a masterpiece such as *War and Peace*, has a perceptive and religious purpose. Ivan Turgenev's novels helped to abolish serfdom.' I even discoursed for twenty minutes non-stop on the differences between pre-revolution Russian literature, and that which came afterwards, such as Sholokhov's *Quiet flows the Don*, and *The Don flows home to the sea.* I really was a somebody on that day. It ended up well too, for Albert, who was waiting for me outside, ready to congratulate or condole, as the result warranted, actually had some money, a 15/- tip. He decided that the occasion called for a celebration, such as a meal out. It was only at Joe Lyons, but actually to have an evening meal out was a rare event. We finished up at our local where not only Albert but the landlord too bought me large glasses of port. It was a super evening; I walked home on air—though my head the next morning was anything but airy.

My Mother, a great reader herself, loved to hear all about my studies. I know that she was really proud that I had the ambition to acquire knowledge. My Father, that quiet and gentle man, had also encouraged me, but for different reasons. Dad believed that all knowledge, however painfully acquired, helped one to live a life that involved all the senses. It made one a complete person, helped one to comprehend the universe and the purpose of life. Mother, and to be honest, I too, at least in the beginning, saw only the material advantages; to lose one's inferiority complex, to be as good as the next person, to become a somebody. Not a very laudable ambition, I know.

But now I lost the best person that ever was, my Father. He slipped out of life as quietly as he had lived it. Mother and I were by his bedside, hoping perhaps for a last word of love. But Dad said nothing. Where he went I know not, but he took a part of Mother and me with him.

For a while Mother even lost her interest in the running of our country. Albert, suppressing his usual antipathy, came to see her much more often. Mother really liked Albert, partly because he too, like Dad, was a quiet man. I'm afraid that Albert never did get really to care for Mother. He found her too dominating and aggressive. Whenever Albert and I had a disagreement, one of the worst things he could say to me was, 'You are getting just like your Mother.' He didn't mean it as a compliment.

However, the Suez Canal affair aroused Mother from her political lethargy. We had ferocious arguments, Mother contending that it was all the fault of America for withdrawing the offer of fifty-six million dollars to help Nasser build the Aswan Dam. I argued with her:

'So why did Britain have to follow suit by withdrawing her offer of fourteen million dollars? France and Britain had no right to attack Egypt; they're plain aggressors. That Anthony Eden seems to have Nasser on the brain. He looks on him as another Mussolini or Hitler.'

Mother's two favourite men were Churchill and Eden. The former because, for her, he had won the war, the latter because he was handsome and looked such a gentleman, unlike such plebeian types as Aneurin Bevan, Attlee and Ernest Bevin. Unfortunately, Churchill had resigned, and now Eden's popularity after Suez had weakened considerably. But Mother had her moment of triumph when she announced, 'Didn't I always tell you that the United Nations would be no more effective than the old League; here they are, assembled to discuss Suez and Nasser, because they think he isn't powerful enough to retaliate; while those barbarians, the Russians, are brutally crushing the Hungarians. But then it's unthinkable that we should go to war with Russia, although there are more Hitlers there than Eden will find in Egypt in a lifetime.'

Albert got annoyed that I argued with my Mother so much. He didn't understand that she really liked to have me disagree; that it gave her pleasure to try to change my erroneous ideas. Albert sat on the fence, saying, with truth, 'It's happened before. In ten years' time it will all be forgotten, some other crisis will fill the news.'

By 1960 we had Macmillan and the affluent society. His slogan 'You have never had it so good', could never have been heard by Albert's firm, for they continued to pay low wages and give the minimum rises. I felt like writing to Macmillan to inform him that for thousands like us his slogan should have been amended to 'You have never had it good'.

'Why don't you?' Albert argued. 'Perhaps he'll send us the money to go on a cruise. Remember how you enjoyed the sea; well, you enjoyed it coming back, when the sea-sick pills combined with whisky knocked you unconscious. Remember it was called a "friendship tour"? How many friends did we make? Everybody was heartily sick of each other by the time we got back. We exchanged addresses with only one couple, and they never wrote.'

'Well, neither did we. It's the same with shipboard romances. They end when the cruise is over.'

Not that I would ever be able to feel romantic on a ship, being one of the worst of sailors. I had premonitions when we boarded at Dover that all would not be well. The ship looked grossly overcrowded, and although I reassured myself that the captain and crew must be on a seaworthy ship, lurid tales of leaky vessels over-insured and sinking while the captain and mate escaped in the only available life-boat, flashed before my eyes. I tried to count the life-boats—it was impossible to count the passengers.

At the same time my vivid imagination could see another *Titanic* drama with me in the rôle of heroine. I hoped that the ship would take a long time to sink, so that half the navy could rush to save us all.

Albert, that great deflater, remarked that we weren't likely to find any icebergs while crossing the English Channel. Albert sometimes gets irritated with me for thinking of such hypothetical situations. Although we hadn't yet left harbour, he wanted to establish himself in a strategic position, while waiting for the bar to open. He certainly had no desire to hear, 'I wonder how we would behave, Albert, if the ship was going down, a plane's engine failed, or an earthquake was imminent? I can't see myself calmly going on knitting, or playing patience, or singing hymns.'

'As to the latter,' said Albert, 'most people would prefer to go down with the ship than have to listen to your singing'—a remark I loftily ignored. I believe my Mother is to be blamed for my dread of the sea. Whenever she had a letter from her brother, who had been a chief engineer on a ship, Mother would sing a melodramatic song about a sea-captain. She always altered the first line so that instead of 'I'll stick to the ship, lads,' it went, 'You stick to the ship lads, I'll save my life; you've no one to love you, I've my children and wife'. I used to weep for those unloved men, left to drown.

Albert got me a job with a retired sea-captain. Though from his general air of raffishness and colourful language, I imagine he was captain only of a banana boat. I'm sure that Albert had no idea of the captain's amorous propensities, he'd only known him for the few hours it took to move him from one house to another in Hove.

I'd left my job at the boarding house; I'd got rather fed up with the grumblings of the boarders, with the plethora of pelvic appurtenances in Mr Trowbridge's room, and especially with Miss Porter's brother. I'd got used to seeing him as a female, but when he-she took up painting, the resultant mess was too much. From the start, all his paintings were of people, and such people. They all looked as though Dracula had been at them, pallid fleshless corpses. He wanted to do one of me, but I refused, not wanting a perpetual reminder that death is just around the corner.

The work was much easier at Captain Owen's than at the boarding house. It always is, working for a man. Very few of them know how housework ought to be done, so if you don't feel too energetic some mornings, a man doesn't notice the difference. Far from being an aloof and silent man of the sea, the captain was loquacious in the extreme. He drank an inordinate amount of rum, a drink I disliked, the smell alone being enough to put me off. However, as I eventually discovered that that was the only drink he had in the flat, I overcame my aversion rather than have nothing. He appeared to have no relatives or friends, and gave me various reasons why. If he was in an uproarious mood he told me he'd 'scuttled' them all, parasites that they were. At other times he would lament that all his family had deserted him. Whether his stories were true or not, they were vastly entertaining. I heard of dusky Polynesian girls, of Java, Fiji, and life in the South Seas. When I asked why he never married, the captain became very sentimental.

'Mrs Powell, I loved only one girl all my life. She was the daughter of a captain, I was second mate. I fell in love at first sight; she really was as Wordsworth wrote, "a phantom of delight ... a lovely apparition", and she was pure.' Here the Captain gave a mighty roar of laughter, saying, 'That was the trouble, she was too bloody pure. I've melted a few in my time, but you couldn't thaw out that ice-maiden. It was all the fault of that she-dragon, her Mother. She brought Celia up with as much meticulous care as though she had spawned a saint, not a flesh and blood female. Celia was an only child, a fact that didn't surprise me, knowing her Father. He cordially disliked all females; I should imagine he had to be bludgeoned to get into bed with one. Celia and I were engaged and still we hadn't got further than holding hands and a chaste kiss. One evening, just after I got back from a six-month trip, I borrowed a car and took Celia out into the country for dinner. After the meal, not forgetting the wine, feeling romantic, and if the truth be told, all agog for love in the physical sense, I stopped the car on the way home, and suggested we sat in the back; which we did. Well, what did that idiotic girl expect? That I would sit there gazing soulfully into her eyes? I'd had too much of that. I began to fondle her in the most delectable places. Mrs Powell, you've never in your life seen anything like it. She literally screamed with horror and revulsion. What the bloody hell have we got it for? I asked her. That was the end of romance for me. Mind you, I may be sixty-nine, but I'm not past it yet. I can still put up a pretty good performance, given the opportunity.'

He took my free hand (I was holding a glass of rum in the other), and sighed sentimentally; at eleven o'clock in the morning. All wasted on me, as I seldom felt like any form of dalliance at that hour of the day. Subtleness being wasted on the Captain, I spelled it out for him. ? SUBTLETY

'Captain Owen, either you want a daily at 4/- an hour, who is here solely to clean your flat; or you need a female who will not only "do for you" but "do" you too on occasions. Well! you may be an inexhaustible Don Juan or Arab sheik in bed, but you are not going to get anybody to share it with you for 4/- an hour. And that's all I want to earn.'

I thought that would be the end of the job, but the Captain just laughed, saying, 'Well, you can't blame me for trying, can you?'

Albert surprised me one day by saying, 'My love, have you noticed that we are losing out in the race for keeping up with the Joneses?'

'I didn't even know we had entered.'

'Well, there are our neighbours each side, both have had extensions built on for proper bathrooms, and we haven't even got a decent bath. Something will have to be done.'

'Fine, Albert, you do have splendid ideas. Perhaps with your eloquence you could persuade the Council to give us the entire grant for a conversion. Tell them we're never going to be able to find our half of the money. Tell them, Albert, that the affluent society has settled either side of us, but a blight has settled in the middle. Don't tell them we are poor, that has no meaning nowadays. Tell them we are deprived and under-privileged. That we have only just graduated from the galvanised bungalow bath to the Heath Robinson contraption that you have fitted up.'

Poor Albert, he did try to improve our house, and often succeeded too. With the old galvanised bungalow bath, after using it we used to open the back door and shoot the water into the yard. But when my brother gave us his old bath, Albert fitted it up in the kitchen near to the sink. The water had to be heated in the wash-boiler, so Albert fitted a rubber tube to the tap, long enough to reach the bath. He then knocked a hole in the wall under the sink for the bath water to run outside, and fitted another rubber tube to the water outlet of the bath. The idea was good in theory. Unfortunately, in practice, these rubber tubes frequently slipped off, flooding the floor.

We now bought, on the never-never, a small square bath. For any couple who liked togetherness in their ablutions it just wouldn't have been large enough. Fitted in by our plumber brother-in-law, free, and covered-in by Albert, nobody could have known it was a bath. We even had a sink water-heater fitted with a swivel pipe that reached the bath. We could have eaten a meal in the time it took to fill, but it was a considerable improvement on using the wash-boiler. The only snag was, that as the bath had not been sunk into the ground, one needed to stand on a chair to climb in, much to the annoyance of my Mother, who at this time had no bath in the council flat, and was looking forward to using ours. I'm not sure that Albert didn't deliberately leave it too high for her.

Fired with enthusiasm at this success, Albert decided that our bit of smelly earth at the back would look better concreted over. We left a corner for Cat, and filled the defunct bath with earth for our herbs. Before cementing Albert buried various old bicycle frames and worn-out tyres. If a future generation ever had a 'dig' there they'd get a surprise. It wasn't Albert's fault that he didn't get the proportions of sand, gravel and cement right, so that the concrete broke up after six months. It could happen to anybody. The concrete was certainly an improvement at first. Albert then bought—also on the never-never—a garden shed; or rather he bought all the necessary stuff to put it up—it being much cheaper that way. 'Can be erected in two hours, simplicity itself, you can't go wrong,' read the advertisement. Unfortunately, there was no Trade Descriptions Act then. For they told lies, you could go wrong, and Albert did. After a whole day he had managed to get the sides up, but he couldn't get the roof on. Something seemed to be missing. Albert's normal good temper most assuredly was. Never being loth to proffer advice, asked for or not, I said to Albert that perhaps the firm had discovered how to overcome the law of gravity. You put the roof up first and then added the rest. I thought I was being funny, but somehow it didn't lessen his exacerbation.

My brother offered to paint the outside of the house if we just paid for the paint. We covered the minute front garden with pink and white slabs, and there we were, as good as the Joneses.

Even our leisure time took on a new dimension, for on one of Albert's jobs he was offered an old television for £5. Not only did it have a much larger screen than our prehistoric set, we could actually see what was on. It was black-and-white instead of being a uniform grey, raining all the time and predisposed to peculiar noises or the picture disappearing.

By now, I'd really acquired delusions of grandeur. I told Albert that our leisure pursuits should be more intellectual, that I knew he didn't want to come to evening classes with me, or read the books I liked, but there must be something we could do together, apart from the usual thing.

'Such as what, Margaret? I'm open to suggestions, just say the word.'

'Well, for a start, we could give up eternally playing solo or crib, for a more intellectual game. One that requires us to use our brains.'

'Have a heart, love. By the time I get home from humping furniture around, I'm tired out. Couldn't we settle for snakes and ladders or ludo? Or just watch our decent telly?'

'Don't be facetious, Albert, I'm serious about this. You never know if it will come in handy. Suppose we got invited out to dinner, and had to play games afterwards? Proper games, I mean.'

'My love, I fail to understand how having the house painted, a proper bath and a telly, is going to result in our being asked out to dinner. We never have been asked yet. Who's going to invite us? We don't know anybody who has people out to dinner.

Your imagination really does run riot.'

Nevertheless, I was determined. However, by the time I had ruled out chess and bridge as being too difficult, and dominoes and darts as too easy, there wasn't much variety left. So we settled for Scrabble. As I could spell and knew more words than Albert, I always won, thus making a harmonious evening. Albert was a lovely partner, he never got angry no matter how often he lost the game. Captain Owen offered to teach me how to play Crown and Anchor, and a game that he called Sailors Sancho; I'd never heard of it, probably his own invention. But I wasn't keen on the former, and far too wary to get involved in some unknown game with Captain Owen. It might have turned out to be a form of strip-poker. As I was always talking about Albert to him—well, I had to keep reminding him that I had a husband —he wanted to meet him at a pub for a chat. I couldn't see that Albert and the Captain would have any common topic of conversation, unless it was me. Besides, it's always best to keep work and pleasure apart.

Albert then had a brilliant idea, well, I thought it a brilliant idea at the time.

'Why don't we, Margaret, while we're watching the telly in the evening, make a wool rug. One of the customers has just finished a huge affair, almost a carpet, in two shades of green. It's really something, she told me it took her a year and was a soothing occupation. We could start off with a fireside rug.'

So we got patterns and eventually decided on a very modern geometric design, bought all the necessary, and got started. The occupation turned out to be as soothing as a thorn under the skin. My fault, I should have known that Albert's enthusiasm wouldn't last out. On any evening that he was home and I wasn't at classes, out would come this bag of wool, and we'd start at opposite ends. What happened? Albert, who was generally dog-tired, either dropped off to sleep, or became so immersed in the telly, that he ceased to work on the rug, much to my irritation.

'Albert,' I'd snap, 'I thought this was supposed to be a combined operation, sharing our leisure and all that. Preparing us for a Darby and Joan existence. It was your idea, you know. It's certainly soothing for you, you're fast asleep in a few minutes— not that you ever needed an opiate to do that. It doesn't soothe me, I'm fuming at my end.' Eventually we gave the whole lot to a hospital to use for occupational therapy. I'd have been there too if we had kept on.

During the last twenty years so many of the old hands had retired that Albert was asked to be a full-time foreman.

'What do you think, my love? It's another pound a week. But with the type of man we have now, the responsibility would be very worrying. Because the job is classed as unskilled, the wages are low and the job is the last resort for a lot of the fellows. They couldn't care less about people's furniture and ornaments. They let it get scratched and chipped, they smoke in the houses, and are barely civil to the customers. Take that job we had the other day. I know the old lady was a bit of an autocrat, but she was a *real* lady. You could tell, well I could, that she had once been a somebody. She wanted the foreman to put dust-sheets down before walking over the carpets, because it was a wet day. All she got was a surly answer. I was so sorry for her. The poor old lady really got in a panic hovering around the foreman, saying, "Please be careful with packing the china, it's been in our family for generations." Looking around the motley crew, I thought, well it won't be for much longer, the generations stop here. So I offered to do the packing—nobody else wanted to do it.'

I question that Albert's work was unskilled; he was really an expert on packing the most delicate stuff. He could have got a job for packing for overseas with more money, but he didn't like changing his job. I advised him not to take on a foreman's job, the extra money was never worth the worry.

Albert came home one day almost in a state of collapse. Not altogether from tiredness, from laughter too. Hastily making him a cup of tea, I sat down to find out why.

'Oh, Margaret, what a day it's been. You'd have died of laughing,' and Albert nearly did just that.

'Get on with it, Albert. I've had nothing here all day to laugh over. The washing machine overflowed all over the floor, the vacuum cleaner has fused all the lights, and the rates have gone up.'

'Well, we had to move this man from his country cottage; there were four of us with the foreman. When we got there, he showed the foreman round, telling him what was to be left in the house and casually added, "and that's all, apart from my goat in the garden." You should have seen our foreman's face, it was a sight for sore eyes. "A goat," he burst out, "we don't move no goats. We don't move no animals except cats or dogs. Look at our official instructions leaflet, it says we move 'household effects'."

' "Sure," answered our customer, "and I also see written on it, 'No gratuities', but I bet that won't stop you accepting a tenner at the end of the job." And at the magic words "ten pounds" our foreman became a different man. We'd have moved a whole farmyard for a tip that size. Before we started, the customer poured us a generous measure of home-made wine. I was prepared to tip mine down the sink unobserved—you know my opinion of home-made wine. But as our customer, Mr Moore, stood with us, I had to drink it. Was it strong? It nearly took the top off my head. Mr Moore said he'd had it for five years to mature it. By the time we had drunk another glassful, I was fit to take on anything.'

'What a pity you couldn't have come straight home after swallowing it,' I murmured, 'you could have ridden the goat home and we could have had a super Walpurgis night.'

Ignoring such frivolity, Albert continued, 'Mr Moore told us that he had to drink goat's milk as a necessary part of his diet. "It's all the fault of my Father, he was the randiest man for miles around. There wasn't a handful of him, but my Mother was his third wife, and he was seventy-four when she had me. My Mother was an educated woman, and she was always telling my Father that he was an old goat and obviously descended from Pan. Father was certainly horny; I reckon he ate goatsbeard—you know, John-go-to-bed-at-noon—for he would have gone to bed—with company—at any time of the day. So when Mother gave birth to me, she was forty then, and I was her only

187

child, the only diet I thrived on was goat's milk. Well, as Mother said, 'it stands to reason.' " '

Pouring out more tea for Albert, and inwardly resolved to start making wine if it did so much for him, I waited for the rest of the tale.

'We went into the garden. There was this nanny-goat, tethered to a post, and Mr Moore had made a wooden crate for its transportation. He got the goat, which he called Millie, into the crate, but just as we were lifting it on to the back of the van, the front opened and out jumped Millie. You never saw such a pandemonium; I've never seen our gang move so fast. That confounded Millie chased us all round the garden. She caught up with old Fred too; we collapsed with laughter. Mr Moore ran after her and Millie broke through the hedge into the next garden. It was a lovely garden too, the owner must have spent hours of labour to get it like that. I thought he'd have apoplexy when Millie started eating his most succulent plants. He jumped up and down with rage, shouting to Mr Moore, "I'll have the law on you, you just wait." Eventually we captured Millie, I'll swear she winked at me, got her into the van, and shut the doors. When we arrived at the other end and opened up, the smell of that goat was enough to knock us out. First thing Mr Moore did was to knock a post firmly into the ground and tether Millie. As he now lives in a row of terrace houses, I don't imagine that the neighbours will consider him and his goat an asset.'

'Well, Albert, I can see that you have had a high old time. And as you have collected all that money, and I've had a foul day, you can take me out this evening, to the theatre.'

'I knew I shouldn't have mentioned the size of the tip,' Albert muttered.

My disastrous day extended into the evening, for the play was one of those actionless talking marathons. I wouldn't have minded if only the cast had not obviously decided that only they needed to hear their conversation—I heard about one word in twelve, even though we had good seats. My pleasure was not further enhanced by Albert's going off to sleep, though I would have put up with it if he had slept quietly. But now and again he gave a terrific snore. I was so embarrassed I wished the earth would swallow him. He only came to life in the intervals, when he managed to be first in the bar. After the theatre—my disposition somewhat soured by now—we had a fish and chip supper in a café, only to sit opposite an ex-Air Force man. I had to sit there while he and Albert went into reams of boring reminiscences. The evening ended for me as foul as the day had been. Still, Albert remained happy, he really does seem to be insulated against outside influences.

It wasn't so much fun at work now as Captain Owen had acquired a lady friend. I shouldn't really have minded, I was there only to clean his flat, not interest myself in his private life. Well, it wasn't exactly private as the lady, big, bouncy and blowsy, was forever drinking gin and draping herself around Captain Owen. No doubt I too could have drunk gin and draped myself around him, but as I would not, I shouldn't have really objected to 'big Bessie', as I called her. But when she took to sleeping in the flat, leaving me to make the beds and put her clothes away, it was too much. So I left that job. Albert was relieved, he had always had qualms over that sea-captain's raf-fishness. I often wondered afterwards whether Captain Owen married Bessie. He certainly bought her gin to drink as she didn't care for rum. But I don't believe she would ever have managed to snaffle him permanently. He was always saying he was just a lone old salt, but he liked it that way. When I told him he had no principles, he informed me that only the rich could afford them.

Especially when Albert was away did he worry about me, and the lack of communications, for naturally we had no telephone. Like the time they moved a very wealthy client to Scarborough and took a week over the job. The usual long-distance driver, who could have plotted the way over the Sahara with just a compass, was in hospital. The new driver couldn't have read a child's primer, let alone a map, and lost the way.

'There we were,' Albert said, 'with a pantechnicon half-full of extremely valuable effects, careering through remote villages and obscure country lanes. That young fellow drove like a Jehu, as though we were being pursued by a gang of thieves. By eight o'clock we still hadn't arrived at Scarborough and the client, who was already there, must have been frantic. By eleven o'clock, in the pitch dark, we drove into a car park in what we assumed was Scarborough, ate the rolls we'd bought on the way, and went to sleep at the back of the van. In the morning, we discovered we were in Bridlington.

'At nine o'clock the next morning, when we reached Scarborough and the house, an extremely hostile reception awaited us. And when the foreman phoned back to the firm to say we had finally arrived, the irate voice over the line nearly blew his ear off.'

On practically every removal job Albert was on, the customer discarded some piece of furniture, and Albert brought it home. Our house was now beginning to resemble a museum—a museum of junk. I was always reading in the glossy magazines that I picked up at work that so-and-so's lovely home was a harmonious mixture of old and new. Somehow it didn't seem to work that way in our old terrace house. It was more a conglomeration than a harmonious assemblage. We had Victorian, Art Nouveau, imitation Jacobean and utility. Nevertheless, although we had few clothes to put into the huge wardrobes, and the solid sideboard was empty, it did fill the house. I didn't in the least mind that visitors thought we were collecting to start our own second-hand furniture business.

I once actually sold one of our pieces for £5—a very elaborate standard lamp, which, as we had no wall plugs, we could never use. I brought a couple home from the first-aid class that I was attending—I had visions of myself as a road-side Florence Nightingale. Mr and Mrs Sheppey were keen on antique furniture, and went into raptures over this lamp. I very much liked Flora, Mrs Sheppey, but he, known as 'Shorty', was a very peculiar individual. Short he certainly was, perhaps that had given him his very self-assertive and aggressive nature. At the first-aid class he was forever asking questions and giving his opinions.

Flora was quite an attractive woman, considerably younger than Shorty, and taller too. One day, when she came to tea on her own, she said to me, 'I bet you have often wondered why I married Shorty. It was because of the tales he told me. I became bemused. And then he seemed so sexy, I didn't know that as well as being short in stature, he was also short in the most important place.'

'Well, he would have to be, wouldn't he? Unless he was all out of proportion.'

'No, not necessarily, Margaret. I had an uncle who was almost a midget, yet he had ten children by a woman twice his size. He had a hard life, as he wasn't short enough to be in a circus, and not tall enough to get the job he wanted. Still, as my aunt always said, "Jeb may not be able to supply me with food, but he can certainly provide the fuel." I only wish Shorty could. When I think of the yarns he stuffed me with, his adventures in Brazil, China and the Seven Seas, all the girls he had—why, he couldn't stuff a rabbit, let alone anything else.'

Here Flora giggled reminiscently, 'But it sure was funny when he used to try. He had passion, while I had pessimism. Which I may say was fully justified.'

Even Albert liked Flora. She always made light of her troubles. Most people only make light of other people's.

Albert was now fast approaching the time when he would have to retire from his removal job. He had been there twenty-two years, and although it was often hard and heavy work, he had enjoyed the life. Where else could he have had such a variety of jobs? Such as when the boss asked who would work on a Sunday removing a bank in Brighton to its new premises. Albert was a volunteer. He had visions of processions up and down North Street, flanked by armed guards, while an admiring crowd looked on. Much to his fury, the money was moved by Security vans; the removal men only had the hard and heavy job of shifting all the office furniture and filing cabinets.

Or the astonishment when they arrived at a place to find they had to move twenty-four babies, fold up twenty-four cots, and empty twenty-four pots. They didn't actually put the babies into the removal van, they went in another vehicle. Or the day they went across to the Isle of Wight on the ferry and the sea was so rough that the valuable things in the van started shifting. The men spent the whole time holding everything together.

Little did I know then that I too would soon be retiring from cleaning and polishing other people's houses. Not that I minded going out to work; some of my jobs provided as much pleasure as profit.

As Albert was for eighteen years a milkman, and for twenty-two years a furniture remover, I do feel that this is an expurgated tale of his life. I reckon that 'true confessions' of all his adventures would perhaps need to be censored.